# Wildflowers

Samantha Roman

Batyah Press

This book is dedicated to Jesus.
Thank You for inspiring all my stories.
To Mommy, Daddy, Journey, and Jose. I love you all!
To every girl with big dreams. Go get 'em!

# Act I: Lights

# Chapter 1: Candy

"THREE CAN KEEP A secret if two of them are dead." Mom took off her purse and looked me straight in the eyes as soon as she entered the kitchen. "Your principal called me at work earlier. You forgot Benjamin Franklin said that?" Her brows furrowed in annoyance. "You scored in the yellow on your practice SATs because of minor mistakes like this." Mom's no-nonsense tone meant her Alcoholics Anonymous meeting had probably challenged her. She walked over to me where I sat at the kitchen table, guitar on my lap and Daddy's old blue travel journal in front of me. I wanted to spend the evening writing lyrics for the song that would hopefully earn us a single with a record company. I didn't want to blow my big chance, but we didn't have a drummer and between the three of us, only Scott and I wrote lyrics. Nina could play anything I sang, but she wasn't a writer.

My defenses rose. "Those were just practice."

Mom dropped her briefcase on the table. "Practice or no practice, I care about how well you do on this test. If you don't score green on the next practice one, I think you might need to take a break from the band just for a bit so you can truly study."

My jaw fell open at the added threat. How could she say that?

"Mom?! Our New York performance is in a few weeks. I can't stop now. We open for *We the Guilty* twice, and Chris said he might even be able to get us to perform in Virginia this spring." I slid out of my chair and walked over to face her at the counter.

Mom let down her hair from her clip and sighed. "And that's another thing. I don't like the idea of this out of state performance with minimum security." She pulled off her heels, washed her hands and began microwaving dinner. "I know you want the big time and all, honey, but your safety comes first, then your school, and finally your recreational activities. Okay?"

I didn't say anything. There goes her anxiety again, ruining my life.

"Understood?" Mom raised an eyebrow and popped the microwave door open.

"Yes." I rolled my eyes and grabbed forks for both of us from the side drawer.

"I agreed to New York since I'm coming with you, but if your next SAT practice scores are in the yellow, you're taking a break. I don't care if Chris has a friend in Nashville, Atlanta, or Los Angeles." Mom sat down across from me at the table.

I wanted to groan, but I caught Mom's firm gaze. My hands grew clammy and I slid them against my jeans. I couldn't risk anything. Couldn't she understand I wanted to be a singer? Daddy would have. I had to make the best of every second now. That included my time at school, so I could score higher and my time with the band, so I could sing my best. I now had to prove I could, in fact, be good at *both* and trust God would give me the big break I'd been praying for.

I hoisted my guitar over my lap and tried to strum as I waited for Mom to finish microwaving her own dinner. I hoped Chris would get us booked at more concerts besides just the one in New York, and we'd become more than YouTube famous. I wished Mom understood college didn't matter that much to me.

We ate the rubbery chicken in total silence, and I considered my future life at college. No one majors in singing. Ever. Music maybe, but not singing. I secretly blamed all Mom's extra attention to my SATs due to her anxiety. She suffocated me with it, more than the apple cinnamon scented hand soap she kept getting for the winter. Even though I'd lived my whole life with her that way, now that she stayed sober, she was never too drunk to miss anything at all. And even though I loved having her back, sometimes I resented her constant and growing "concern."

That night, I flipped through the pages of my new youth group journal. We'd been tasked with practicing the Fruit of the Spirit. As a new Christian, I wanted to bear all the fruit I could. Showing love and joy onstage should be easy, if Mom would just let me perform, right? Kindness to fans, goodness to my fellow fans and patience with myself when I made mistakes. God wanted me onstage. I could tell. I slid the journal into the nightstand drawer and shimmied under my covers. This was one challenge that was practically in the bag.

# Chapter 2: Leslie

I FISHED MY PHONE out of the toilet. *Great,* I thought, shaking it off. Now I'd either have to get it repaired or buy a new one. I glanced at myself in the mirror that Tuesday morning and began washing the residue of toilet water off my hands. There was no way on the planet I'd ever tell high-strung Mike from Rob's finance and land acquisition department his call had been disconnected because his boss accidentally knocked her phone into the toilet while doing her makeup.

I pulled my hair into a French twist and hurried down the steps to send Mike an email from my laptop: "We'll catch up later." I had to meet with the mayor today. I was just opening up my laptop to message Mike and confirm my Rosewater meeting, when the doorbell rang. When I answered it, there was Anna Anderson. She was the sister of the boy who had killed Rob and the girl who'd gotten pregnant not too long after the accident.

"Hi, Ms. Leslie. Do you have a minute?" Anna's bump showed a little despite her baggy sweater. I motioned for her to step inside.

"I really appreciate you paying for everything to help take care of me and the baby." Anna didn't remove her coat. I sat down on the bench in the hallway, a little breathless from my morning whirlwind, and patted a spot next to me. She gingerly accepted.

"My parents tell me if I want to keep the baby, I'll have to move out since I'm turning eighteen this summer. But, I can stay home if I give up the baby and go to community college."

I eyed her closely. *Where was this going?* I watched as Anna played cat's cradle with her fingers.

"I was wondering if you would consider taking my baby?" she sputtered, looking right into my eyes. "I mean, if he or she would have a shot at having a better life, it would be with you. I mean...I know you're doing a lot by picking up the bill and everything. I just wondered..." She vigorously rubbed her hands together, untangling the nerves that bundled inside the warm home.

Like broken puzzle pieces, my heart shattered and my throat closed from pure emotion. My mind raced back to Robert Jr., the night his tiny body was alive, his heart beating against my chest for only minutes before he grew cold. My third angel baby. And now, here stood my last chance at having a new baby. I didn't realize how huge that empty hole had become. It was three sizes too large. I lowered my head to hide the unplanned tears.

"I know my family hurt yours a lot..." Anna's face turned red. "And I've been rude to you in the past. I just thought maybe-" She started crying, and I let some silent tears fall too. The baby had nothing to do with the past, but it had everything to do with the future. A future where I finally snuggled a precious infant close again and heard tiny little sighs. A tiny flutter of fear skipped across my heart as I worried if the baby would live or if I'd have to take yet another loss. My mind swirled in a twisted shade of gray as I remembered all the dark days crying by an empty crib. Clasping her hands in mine to shake the feeling, I said, "I'd be happy to take him or her. Don't worry about anything." I imagined Chris would be okay with it. Now that we'd officially started dating, I had to keep him in mind for all major decisions, especially one of this size. He'd mentioned wanting to have a son in past years, but I'd have to ask him to make sure.

Anna let out a long sigh. Candy would finally be getting the baby I'd promised her, and I knew she'd be the best big sister in all of Honeybrook. I leaned over and hugged Anna close.

"Take care of yourself," I whispered, "and keep me posted."

Anna let a smile cross her face as we both stood and she headed for the door. "I will."

I held the large oak door open for a moment after she left and let it all sink in. I was going to be a new mom again? A thrill of excitement filled me and I couldn't stop smiling. I quickly went back upstairs and scanned the hallway for the unused guestroom a few doors down from Candy's room. I walked into the huge room that had a closet and a window overlooking the beach. I let out a tiny laugh. This could work, and I could decorate a new nursery!

❖❖ — ◆ ◆ — ❖❖

"Here's the new phone you asked for." Susan sat in my office and handed me my new phone with the ugliest case I'd ever seen. Orange. No designs, just shiny, neon orange. It may have been the perfect case for Scott, but not exactly my speed. Maybe Chris would like it. He'd given me the cutest winter paperweight for my home office this past weekend, complete with a snowy January scene and a cardinal. We'd gone on lunch dates, coffee dates, then official dinner dates. He'd been on my mind so much more lately because of his kindness over the last few months. Even the paperweight was cuter than this phone case. I wanted to pick out something for my guy this weekend and smiled to myself. I could tie it in with the baby suggestion.

"Thank you," I told Susan as I popped my phone into the new case. It squeaked as I shoved it in, making me dislike it even more. I'd have to get a different color case before Friday.

"No problem," Susan smiled at me. "And don't forget your shoes."

I stopped twisting in my chair. "What time is it?"

"The mayor is here and your heels are in the corner." Susan stood to leave, and I hurried to slip on my lavender heels. Ones that did not in the least bit match my new phone. I walked over to Rob's old office for the meeting and discreetly hid the phone in the pocket of my blazer. How I ended up with an orange-cased phone after my old one got clogged with toilet water was not the conversation I wanted to have.

"Good morning, Mayor," I acknowledged the balding man.

"Leslie, I thought we were on the same page now." Mayor Rosewater sat where he'd angrily splashed coffee on me years ago. "We don't do affordable housing, and we won't talk about eighty-million-dollar mistakes. Or any other mistakes. And could you be ever so kind as to explain to me how this project wouldn't lose you money?"

"Mayor, this project means a great deal to me," I said, reflecting on Rob, our shared dream, and our legacy. Maybe some people didn't want to work with me, but maybe some people believed in the same thing I did—second chances. I traced the floorplan that sat on my desk with one finger and didn't make eye contact with the mayor.

"I've had the sinkhole safely filled, and if you can grant us the proper zoning, I'd love to offer affordable homes to families in the spring."

"It doesn't work like that, Leslie, and you know it." The mayor shook his head at me. "After twenty years, you should know. We've had this conversation before." The mayor slid his annual meeting schedule on top of the housing plans. Usually, the January list came stacked with quarterly meetings that Rob and I would have attended and a few dates for finalized decisions from his office. Maybe a City Hall meeting? I put on my readers and began to review it. Four meetings for the first half of the year?! Just for him to hopefully approve my planning? My heart sank and a sense of dread crawled up my neck. What was he about to do now that Rob was gone?

"I know in some states the town council gets involved." I tried to make sense of everything and take control of the situation.

The mayor's forehead began to sweat. "I make the decisions around here, and no, I will not involve the town council. The answer is and still will be no."

"Mayor," I said, shifting in my chair, "Honeybrook has hardworking people who work almost an hour from where they live." I thought about Susan and Jack. "Don't we at least have a moral obligation to help?"

The mayor stayed seated, but looked around in his chair as if searching for something. "Phew, I'm still in America. So no, I have no moral obligation to do anything. Is that all you needed to know, Leslie? I guess Rob handled these things more than you, so maybe you're just not used to it."

Heat rose in my chest and my hands grew warm. No wonder the mayor dripped with sweat. The air conditioning needed to be checked. "Mayor, with all due respect, it is my property, and as a developer, I need to reach an agreement with you on what the land will be used for. I build homes for a living, so we have to decide what kind of homes are going to go there."

"Leslie, what's wrong with exclusive single-family homes starting from the $800s?" Mayor Rosewater asked.

I stood, demanding control. "I'm not accepting this as your final answer, Mayor" I told him. "Somewhere you know that answer is wrong. And why are we meeting so much anyway?"

"I knew you'd say that, and I'll meet with you again, Leslie, according to schedule. But the answer will be no again, so don't get your hopes up. And that little paper should help you stay organized, as we iron out the finer details by the second quarter."

I bit my lip. "If you don't grant me zoning, anyone who dies because of the cold this winter will be on your hands."

"What, do you want a homeless shelter too?"

I narrowed my eyes at him. "I want everyone in Honeybrook to have a fair chance. Isn't that what everyone deserves?"

Mayor Rosewater tossed his head back and started laughing at me. "Rob must have had you working with him just so he could enjoy working with his wife. You purchased a sinkhole, Leslie, a sinkhole! And now you want to sell lower priced homes to be nice? What were you as a kid? A Girl Scout? Let's not forget I knew you before you married Rob."

I bit my tongue so hard it hurt. If he would make it this hard for me, I'd have to figure out another way to keep Rob's dream alive. I'd almost killed it with the sinkhole disaster, but at least now I had another chance. And I couldn't lose that. My phone rang. I checked it and stifled a groan. Mike. "Can we continue this conversation?" I asked.

"We always have," the mayor sneered at me as he stood to leave. "But let's not kid ourselves, Leslie. Rob's not here anymore to protect you, and maybe when I keep saying no, you'll get the message."

I shuddered, but still shook his hand. "I can only do my best for the people of Honeybrook, Mayor."

The old man rolled his eyes. "Let me be crystal clear, Leslie. Like I said before, Rob's not here, but my brother Sam is still in charge of organizing music festivals on the East Coast. You and Candy should be careful." He stood at the entrance to my doorway. "Since we have four meetings, there's still unfinished business, isn't there?" He tightened his coat and left.

Somewhat unnerved, I left the room, walked back to my own office, and grabbed my water bottle. "I guess that's it, Susan. Thanks." I snapped my briefcase shut after the grueling meeting. I glanced at the clock. Twelve-thirty. "I won't be in tomorrow, but I'll call you about the updates we discussed." I planned to have lunch with Chris and gently ask him what he thought about taking Anna's baby. Then, if he said yes, go shopping for the new baby and spend the evening talking to Candy about the idea. My heart ached from wanting a baby again. From my window, I caught a glimpse of the pompous mayor strutting to his car and backing away. He'd made motherhood hard for me in the past, with insane demands and meetings that forced me to take Candy everywhere I had to go. He might make life very hard on me and the new baby too.

"Yes, ma'am." Susan handed me my coat.

I slid it on slowly. "Thank you."

# Chapter 3: Candy

"**S**TAND WHERE YOU ARE," I told Scott in the school hallway and circled him in a hug. Then I pulled out my cell phone to snap a selfie of the two of us.

"I need to update your picture in my phone," I winked at him.

Scott grinned back. "Text that picture to me so that way we match."

I felt myself growing warm as I sent him the picture. Scott said the sweetest things. I twisted the ring he gave me around my finger and smiled. Nina approached us at the lockers.

"Hey, practice tonight, right?"

"Yeah," I whispered, "I'm so excited to sing and not think about school or SATs at all."

Scott smiled at me. "Same here."

"See you at practice?" I gave him a huge smile and shoved my hands into the burgundy hoodie he'd given me last year.

"You bet." Scott gave his hair a quick toss, then left for his class. I bit my lip as I thought about how much I liked...actually loved...him. My adorable, precious Scott. I swiped my phone open so I could see our picture again and pressed it against my chest. Just two hours until band practice!

# Chapter 4: Leslie

B RIEFCASE PACKED, PURSE IN hand, I turned around and noticed a gray wisp of smoke coming from my interior window that faced the offices and breakroom. I thought I'd placed a no-smoking policy last month.

"Did I send the no-smoking update?" I asked Susan.

"Yes."

"Then why–" I froze as I heard a heart-stopping thud followed by a shout. If I had remote doubts about worrying, the terror on Susan's face confirmed them. And then I heard another yell. This wasn't a random employee caught taking a quick smoke in the bathroom. I started to rush into the hallway, but just as I stepped out, the breakroom door burst off its hinges, missing me by only a few feet. I heard Susan beside me, already sobbing. I clenched my jaw and moved a little further to investigate, but stopped as a toaster flew through the air, exploding into flames. People ran for cover.

Cold horror shot through my veins, and I wanted to move, but I couldn't. This building, the last part of the company that I had of Rob, wobbled before my eyes in the heat. Flames licked up the green, carpeted floor and came closer to me and Susan.

Susan grabbed my phone for me and bolted for the stairs. "Come on!"

I snapped to my senses, ran back to my office, and pressed the emergency button under my desk. "Coming!"

As I ran down the hallway, the fire roared closer, devouring staff and family pictures off the walls, desks, chairs, and everything else in its path. I stumbled after Susan, sweating and hating my heels with a passion. I worried they might melt to my skin, so as I stood at the top of the steps, I yanked them off and tossed them through a vacated office window being consumed by the deadly flames. Everyone crammed into the staircase, and the intense heat from the fire created a wobbly shield around us.

*I could die,* I thought while listening for the fire sirens, but heard none. *I might die right here today.* Black smoke billowed above me as burning wood crackled and fell from the third floor. I felt like I was standing inside the color picture of the boating accident I'd received in a newspaper article in 1993. The picture captured every fear I ever had–losing everything that mattered. Now, after rebuilding my whole life and making new things matter, the fire seemed to reach for my soul and threaten to take almost all that mattered again. I thought about how my parents must have been scared during their last moments, gasping for air. The heat from above made everything wave in front of me, almost like the suffocating waves from the boating accident. I tried to make my way down the narrow staircase, but I couldn't. My employees were bottlenecked at the bottom, and I kept trying to keep my head below the smoke and flames. I tried not to inhale the smoke, but being surrounded by dozens of people made that impossible as I stayed trapped in the hot staircase, barefoot, and gripping onto a wooden railing I knew would soon burn. Even the wood beneath my feet started to warm as I pushed forward, while every human

I'd ever hired shoved their way down four flights of stairs to the bottom.

Mike kept shouting at people to move and I noticed Jack, Wendy, and a few others fleeing behind him. My body started to quake as my hopes and dreams started to physically crash around me.

After what felt like an eternity, we all made it to the last flight of steps. My toes ached from being stepped on, and I was struggling to breathe and falling behind. I looked up through one of the interior windows just in time to see Candy's old homeschool room and her old pink notebooks crash through the ceiling. One of her notebooks landed on a smoldering pile of paper and burst into flames. I wished I knew how to pray. As Candy's notebook disintegrated, I wished to see my daughter one last time. Smoke filled my lungs and I gasped for air. The entire left side of the building started to crumble, and more fiery beams of wood fell to my side as I tried to follow the crowd. Broken bits of plaster rained down like sprinkles, powdering my face with even more dust. My bare feet collected dozens of scratches only I could feel. I'd gone numb as the nightmare unfolded. Where were the firefighters? Would I see Candy again?

The last beam fell directly in front of the last step, but I stretched one leg over the scorched wood and jumped over it, ripping my skirt in the process. One more thing ruined as I found myself surrounded by dancing flames that only reminded me of the day I lost my parents. I saw rain begin to pour outside, and I feared Candy might officially lose both of her parents too. But now, fear had a smell. A sulfuric, awful smell with a roaring sound I'd never forget. My heart raced as I searched the room for the screaming person, but couldn't find him or her. Did my parents scream like that? Still behind my frantic staff,

I leaned against a wall and tried to catch my breath. It burned my back and I tried to move with the crowd, pushing my way forward, but without much success. I thought about going out the back door, but people were pouring outside in both directions, trying to escape.

More flames started to cover the enormous lobby on the first floor, making it almost impossible to reach the door. *Will I make it out?* The second floor let out a groan and my heart sank as more wooden beams started to fall. Thick, dark smoke blurred my vision, and I stumbled for a new, clear space behind the front desk so I could get a clear view of the exit. Both doors had been melted off and flames leapt around the exits. I glanced at the window. There were no firefighters and no help. The crib from Robert Jr.'s nursery fell within my view, as if it were a cruel joke. All I ever had was hope, and now I only hoped to survive. The glass window panes curled as they succumbed to the fire, but I still refused to give up.

"Help!" I shouted into the darkness, hoping at least a firefighter would pull me out of the corner I'd worked myself into– a granite, fireproof front desk. "Help!"

But like I feared, there was the crackling of burning wood, followed by a few embers, then silence.

# Chapter 5: Candy

"**C**AN WE GIVE YOU a lift home from school?" Scott asked after practice. "It's raining."

I glanced at Mrs. Carrington in the minivan as I got in. "Thanks."

"We have to stop by the office," Mrs. Carrington said. "Drew's car is being serviced, and I have to pick him up too."

"Okay." I settled into the backseat and strapped on my seatbelt. I re-tied the bow on the back of my knee-high boots since they'd come undone in the after-school shuffle. I was glad for the ride. In just the few minutes I'd been in the car, it had started raining harder. Scott and his mom were laughing about something that had happened at school when we turned the corner to the office. The first thing I saw was the bright red firetruck. I saw firefighters outside of the building and clouds of smoke filling the air. I bolted upright, knocking my elbow into the door handle, and Mrs. Carrington gasped. They directed us away from the parking lot.

My heart leapt into my throat. "What just happened?" I whispered as we pulled into the adjacent lot. Paramedics and police officers swarmed Chancellor Homes. Men and women wearing red, heavy gear trudged about, some carrying hoses, others helping soot-covered workers. They were scattered around, rescuing people who'd left fire to stand in the rain. *Where's my mom?* My heart almost thudded out of my chest as I took in the living nightmare with my own eyes. Hundreds of people were screaming, sounding like Doomsday, but none of those people were my mom.

"Stay in the car," Mrs. Carrington unbuckled and reached for her phone, dialing Mr. Carrington, her eyes moist as she did. "Let me ask. Everyone is probably shuffled around." She sounded like she was trying to convince herself more than me.

"No way!" I yelled back, leaning forward. "I need to find Mom." I hopped out of the van and ran towards the building.

Before my boots even hit the sidewalk in front of the building, a female firefighter stepped in front of me and grabbed my arm. "Hey, you can't go in there."

I reached for my phone and almost dropped it, but steadied my hand as I dialed Mom's cell phone. "You've reached Leslie Chancellor. I'm sorry I can't come to the phone."

"This isn't happening," I muttered under my breath. I tried again. No answer. I dialed the house.

"You've reached the Chancellors." The rain pelted my face as I tried one last time. People screamed as they ran past me and my heart sped up. The phone rang for a little longer, but no answer. I dialed her cell in a last-ditch effort as a swarm of people, one of them Wendy, left the building. But still no Mom. Wendy's coughing reminded me of how much Mom already coughed. The rain soaked my clothes as I moved closer to the melted door. Mom must still be inside. And no one helped her get out?

"God, please help me find my mom," I whispered.

The firefighters had put out some of the flames out-side and around the door, but from the way fire still leapt and danced in the windows, I knew a fire still raged inside. Scott sidled up next to me.

"Find our parents?"

"Guys, whoever you're looking for should be on their way out," the same firefighter told us.

"It's my mom," I choked out the words. "She has COPD."

The woman's face changed. "We have people inside doing a sweep. They'll pull her out."

"Alive?"

She said nothing for a moment, then tilted her hel-met back and said, "We hope so."

"I have to go in!" I screamed, shaking in fear as I forced the words out. "She's all I have."

"You can't, honey, I'm sorry," The firefighter said. "It's not safe." She pulled me back a little, then turned away to use her walkie talkie.

In that brief second as she turned, I escaped her sight and got closer to a window entrance. I squinted my eyes at the enormous billows of smoke and sucked in a final breath of damp, January air. Out of the corner of my eye in the next parking lot over, I saw the dark outline of Mayor Rosewater, observing the flames devouring our legacy. At my feet laid an orange phone with a cracked screen. The song Mom used as her ringtone stopped my heart for all of one second, and I bent down to pick it up. Mike. I didn't answer. A flame kindled inside me. I looked at Scott and we both nod-ded. We hadn't seen my mom or Mr. Carrington. No one was looking, and no one was helping our parents. Scott squeezed my hand as we stood outside the burnt window frame, wide enough for the both of us.

"God, help me," I prayed one last time as we both took a step between life and death.

# Chapter 6: Leslie

"**M**OM!" I HEARD CANDY'S distinct panicked voice above the noise.

*No*, I ducked as yet another lighting fixture crashed to the ground and my heart fell to my feet. *Who let my daughter in a fiery building?*

"Mom!?" she called again, and this time I saw the outline of her petite frame.

I anxiously searched for some way to escape the leaping flames. The curve around the service desk provided some sort of an angle I might be able to climb over before Candy came too close. Or maybe I could crawl on top of it.

"Stay where you are!" I shouted back. Candy was all that mattered now, and I wasn't about to lose her today. "Get out!" I took what I considered the last sight of my perfect child. "Listen to me!"

Candy defiantly raced toward me, with Scott in tow. My hands quaked as Candy ran closer to the flames, and I couldn't take my eyes away to make sure she stayed safe. But Candy grabbed one arm and Scott's strong, firm hand clenched my other, and they yanked me over the service desk. Scott gave me one final heave over the beam that had trapped my escape, a heave so hard I felt like my shoulder was coming out of its socket. I fell into Scott, shaking. The air was getting hotter. Just as I threw out my hand to grab Candy's, she shrieked and collapsed underneath another beam. *We would die here after all,* I thought, as my world went black.

# Chapter 7: Candy

"THAT'S A PRETTY BAD burn," the doctor told me. "You should have let the firefighters get your mom out. They're trained for it... and dressed for it."

I swiped at the ashes on my smoke-covered sweater. "I had to," I sobbed. "I couldn't lose anyone else."

He cocked his head to the side. "What do you mean?"

"I lost my daddy in an accident. I had to at least try."

The doctor grew silent.

"How's Mom?"

"She inhaled a lot of smoke, honey," he began, "and that's not good for anyone. For someone with your mom's condition, that's even worse."

"How much worse?" I painfully scooched up in my bed.

"She was trapped. COPD only gets worse, and your mom already struggled. They had to intubate her." The doctor pressed a stethoscope to my chest. "She couldn't breathe well enough on her own when she got here, so she can't talk with the tubes at the moment."

My heart fell to the pit of my stomach as I tried to imagine Mom with a tube in her mouth, unable to talk. Tears sprang in my eyes, and the burn on my leg started to hurt even more.

"How's Scott?" I asked.

"I'm not at liberty to say," The doctor replied, standing at the door to leave. "He told me you two weren't related."

My turn to fall silent. I wondered how his dad and Ms. Susan fared in the fire. They were a community, almost family. I had always known Mom thought of the office as her second home. Or at least, it used to be.

Nurses entered and went to work cutting off my blood-soaked jeans, while more techs caused me excruciating pain as they cleaned my relatively large wound with strong disinfectant. The last swipe down my leg stung the most, and I released a scream into the thin hospital pillow, gripping the sheets as if my life depended on it. I stared at my burned calf and the messy bandages that covered it. It looked nasty, and I didn't want to think about how bad it would look once it healed. Even with the bandages, blood had soaked through yet again.

The burn stopped just short of needing a skin graft, but it would leave a scar. I fell back against my pillow and scrunched my eyes in pain as the nurse wrapped my leg in gauze a second time.

"Hey, honey." Chris surprised me as he walked in the door cautiously, his eyebrows lifted in concern. "How are you feeling?"

"It hurts," I stifled sobs. "How did you hear about the fire?"

"It's the only thing on the local news. I stopped in to visit your mom, but it looks like she might stay here for a while longer."

I cleared my dry throat, and I realized I'd been pretty blessed not to be intubated at this precise moment. Sure, I hurt, but I could breathe. Somewhere in the same hospital, my mom was fighting to do the same.

"When you're discharged, I'll give you a lift home," Chris continued. "Your mom is going to need more time."

The thought of us being separated again crushed me somewhere so deep, I thought I'd break. I'd fought for us to be together, through actual flames! Now, I'd have to wait until the doctors felt Mom could come home. It seemed like we could never find normal.

# Chapter 8: Leslie

"COPD IS DIFFERENT FOR everyone," Dr. Peters, my pulmonologist, told me as I wiped soot from my face. Removing the tube had been painful, and it felt like sandpaper on the inside of my throat. Yet, lying on the scratchy sheets, I tried to focus on his face instead of the pain.

"What are you saying?"

"With the damage that happened to your lungs a few days ago, we'd like to keep you for the rest of the week."

"Rest of the week? Did I pass out? How long have I been here already? Where's my daughter? There's more, isn't there?" I fiddled with the nasal cannula in my nose. "Tell me."

"You've passed out a few times, but you've stayed with us and are getting better. A friend named Chris Schaeffer took your daughter home yesterday," he reassured me. "Candy acknowledged she knew him and identified him as her godfather."

I sighed in relief.

"Some people don't escape fires, and you're blessed to be alive." Dr. Peters and I locked eyes, and my heart skipped a beat out of fear when I saw his forehead wrinkle with unease.

"What's happening to me next?" I clutched my sheets tighter.

Dr. Peters lifted his eyebrows in worry and took one of my hands into his. "Your lungs were severely injured in the fire." He inched closer, and I felt fear tingle in my fingertips. "Do you even remember us bringing you here?"

I shook my head no, realizing that I must have forgotten memories from the times I'd blacked out. "I just remember my building being on fire."

"Thank God you got here in time, but your oxygen levels are so low that I don't want to give you a sense of false hope."

"So, am I dying?" I whispered and glanced at the machines around me, not sure if the beeping or the numbers were good or bad. My throat filled with emotion, and I squeezed the metal railing of the bed. A nurse entered pushing a cart of sorts, and I hoped the needles weren't meant for me.

"No, but the injury was pretty bad. You'll need to use oxygen therapy to help you breathe like you should, but, Leslie, it's a miracle you made it down four flights of stairs with that much smoke inhalation in the first place."

*On oxygen?!*

"Will I–" I stopped to cough. It was different than before, harder if that were possible. I couldn't stop. The nurse quickly gave me a pink bucket to catch the surprisingly enormous amount of mucus.

"Yes, that will be worse for a bit, and you'll need to rest for a while. That means no working." Dr. Peters raised an eyebrow at me. "I mean it. No working. No traveling. Healthy food. Good sleep." He examined me and pressed on my middle. I let out an unexpected yelp.

"I'm going to give you something for that too. The stress of it all is eating at your stomach again."

I slumped deeper into my pillow. I had to rebuild an empire of an office while I was falling apart? What did God want from me? I gave Him my husband and three kids. What next? I let the tears wash the smudges of smoke from my face as I thought of how I'd need help managing an oxygen tank and keeping the air clean. There'd be more inhalers and a heavy cough, in addition to my existing anxiety. Those things would challenge and change life for Candy and me all over again.

# Chapter 9: Candy

BECAUSE I STAYED OVERNIGHT in the hospital, I also spent the next day home from school. I had a limp and a doctors' note to take care of my burn from home a little longer. Chris came over that same afternoon so I could visit Mom. As I scurried around the house getting ready to go, I finally found my phone in my purse. I had two unanswered phone calls from Scott! I'd almost forgotten. My brain flooded with a cool relief that he'd called. He'd made it home too. I had to call him as soon as I got back home. I promised myself. *He'd probably called to find out how I'd made out since the doctors didn't share information with either one of us,* I thought as I got into the car with Chris and we drove the seven-minute drive to the local hospital.

"The doctor told me Mom's had a really rough go of it," Chris said as we pulled into the parking lot. "She's been asking to see you for hours on end." Chris' face softened a little as we both got out of his Lexus.

As soon as we walked into room 205, I wanted to run away. I didn't want to know what the doctors would say, or if Mom had bad news for me. Worse anxiety? Worse COPD? Worse both? I held my breath and pushed my way through the blue striped hospital curtain.

"My baby." Mom's voice was hoarse as she reached for me, letting the IV tubing dangle over the bedrail. I immediately hugged her, and she squeezed me back. Chris leaned in for a hug too.

"How are they treating you, Mom?" I asked.

"I couldn't breathe," Mom sighed.

A doctor walked in and placed a hand over Mom's hand. "Mom gets to hang out with us for a little while longer until we can get her cough under control and some solid food in her stomach."

"What do you mean?" Chris asked. "She already has a cough."

"It's gotten a lot worse. And paired with the panic attacks she's experiencing, she couldn't keep breakfast down." The doctor squeezed Mom's hand. "Maybe having you guys here will help."

Mom's eyebrows formed a saddened V, but she motioned for me to join her on the bed. "I have to keep these." She pointed to the tiny tubes in her nose.

The tubes in Mom's nose seemed to shiver, and my heart sank to my feet. Oxygen? Mom brushed my arm with her hand as if to reassure me.

"The fire caused permanent damage." Mom adjusted the tubes a little. "How did you make out, honey?"

Chris sat down across from us, and the doctor clicked away at the computer.

"I burned my leg." I showed her my scar, and she immediately gasped.

"Do you have ointment for that?"

A nurse walked in with a tray of food for Mom, interrupting us. "Perfect timing," the doctor said as he stood from his stool. "Lunch should go better, okay?"

Chris looked at me and I looked at Mom.

"My lungs were already in a bad spot." Mom moved a saltine cracker back and forth on her tray with one finger and didn't make a motion to eat her soup. "The fire basically solidified matters." She turned her head and began coughing forcefully. The nurse provided her with a small tissue.

"I'm not contagious," Mom said and offered a weak smile before hugging me. "Did you want any of this?" She pointed to the packaged cookies on her tray.

I bit my lip at the sight of the dusty two-pack. "It's okay," I said.

"I didn't know you guys were the Chancellors." The doctor gave us warm smiles. "When I pulled up your mom's chart, I thought to myself, we have the Chancellors here? The homebuilders?" he gave me a wink. "I didn't believe it until I heard your mom's accent."

Mom laughed her signature, high, tinkly laugh, and I relaxed a little.

"You can take the girl out of the country, but you can't take the country out of the girl." Mom winked at me.

"You cannot," Chris said and nodded his agreement from his spot.

"But, you were Leslie St. John, right?" the doctor asked. "If you were from here originally? Did I go to school with you?"

Mom paused and looked at me. "Yes." She cleared her throat, opened the ice pop on her tray and began to suck on it slowly.

"I thought so." The doctor stiffened and gave me a side-eye expression, as if I were now a bad guy because of the St. John heritage, and my heart went ice cold. My eyes locked into his, and he changed his face quickly. "I hope you get well soon, Leslie. If I don't see you when you're discharged, I hope you have a good recovery."

I no longer trusted him with Mom.

"You won't be back?" Mom asked.

"I have a few weeks off. I'll probably take the boat out and do some winter fishing. Work can be stressful, as you know, I'm sure." He and the nurse left the room, and I looked at Mom, grateful the doctor wouldn't be "caring" for her anymore.

"Tim wanted to join the military," mom smiled. "But he could never lose the weight." Mom shifted in her bed a little and winced.

"Did you need water?" Chris asked her.

Mom smiled with her eyes. "I'm fine, just uncomfortable because I have to keep the tubes since breathing is going to be much harder now. And apparently I'll cough more, and I'm at a higher risk for infections, and blah, blah, blah." Mom ran her fingers through my hair. "At least I can hopefully work remotely to supervise the office being restored to its original glory."

Chris' facial expression softened. "Sure, after you take it easy for what, a month?"

"We go to New York for Candy's concert." Mom blinked at both of us. "In however many days that is."

I bit my lip. I'd prayed for success and a beautiful first out-of-state concert, but at what cost to Mom?

❖❯❯⋯⋯•♦•⋯⋯❮❮❖

That afternoon, I called Scott, but he didn't answer.

"Hey, Scott, this is Candy. I misplaced my phone after the fire, and I'm sorry I missed your call. Give me a call when you can." I hung up, hoping he was okay. I considered walking over, but my leg hurt so much it was out of the question. I searched the kitchen for the ointment I'd been given to help it heal.

That night, I sat at the kitchen table and called him again. Still no answer. I chewed my lip. They told me he had survived...right?

# Chapter 10: Candy

CHRIS BROUGHT MOM HOME the next day, and the flowers he had for her brought out her tinkly laugh again. I didn't realize I'd been holding my breath for what seemed like ages. The moment she walked in, I went to hug her, despite her record setting frazzled hair and smelly clothes. Now, this time we both flopped down on the couch. Mom wore oxygen tubes in her nose as promised, and my eyes watered.

"I can't leave you two alone, can I?" Chris smirked at both of us.

Mom's gentle expression showed her gratitude, and we both knew it hurt her to say much. But she did talk to me.

"Thank you for coming inside, Candy. I don't think I had it in me to crawl any further."

"I'd do it again." I propped my leg up on the coffee table. "We're all we have."

"I know," Mom whispered. She adjusted a tiny purse-like tank of oxygen next to her.

Chris fixed breakfast for us, but I ate only half since my concern about Mom had actually started to grow since she came home. Because of my burn, I couldn't shower normally yet, but Mom looked like she needed a complete makeover.

# Chapter 11: Leslie

T HAT FRIDAY, I SAT on my couch and faced my rehab therapist. I wasn't used to these sessions and didn't really like them, but as a part of healing from addiction and now from a fire, I'd promised Chris and Candy I would. So, here I sat, iced coffee in my bruised hand, waiting for Trish to say something.

"I feel like you're making some progress." Trish's voice came out warm.

I swished the ice around in my cup and looked down. "I don't know what you're saying."

"We've talked about what has led up to your habits and how you're going to face your new challenges. You've been handed a lot of new challenges and some blessings. You said you really feel like you are falling in love with Chris."

I smiled. "I didn't see it coming." From the heat in my cheeks, I knew my face had to have that romantic glow. "We've been friends forever."

Trish adjusted her dreadlocks and gave me a wink, her purple eyeshadow shimmering. "Love blooms at the most unexpected times, but with that being said, why won't you share your deepest roots with me?"

"Deepest roots?" I wrinkled my nose at her.

"Yes," she sighed. "There had to be something before the lost building, the lost babies, before you lost your husband, and possibly even before your parents." Trish started prodding me. "What happened that you can still feel to this day?"

I shifted positions in my chair. "It all starts with losing my parents," I lied.

Trish leaned forward. "But you keep saying it wasn't an accident, Leslie. Who do you blame? You're sober, but you're a pile of nerves, and there's someone out there you blame for a lot of things. Who is it?"

I tightened my lips and didn't say anything. Even if it was just to my therapist, I didn't want it coming back on Candy. Most people don't know small towns have rules. Like each family is known for what they've done or are doing. For instance, the Rosewaters always scorch earth. Whoever is responsible for the death of one of their own brings destruction to their entire household. But the St. Johns had history with them, and Rob wasn't here to protect me.

❧ ⋯ ✦ ⋯ ❧

Later that afternoon, I stood in the bathroom wanting to change from my therapy outfit to something safe and comfortable for when Chris came over to check in. I held tightly to a blue hoodie from New Life University. Mom and Dad had purchased it for me during new student orientation.

"Blue is your color," Mom told me as we left the campus store. "It brings out your eyes."

"I know we're just a flight away." Dad hugged me as we walked across the lush campus. One hand in his pocket fingered the deck of cards I knew he always carried. His other arm wrapped around me. "But even though we're hours apart, let this hoodie remind you of the hugs waiting for you back home." Dad's eyes flitted back and forth, as if waiting for someone or something, and I followed his gaze. Seeing nothing, I hugged him in front of the old, brick science building.

The soft, fleece hoodie felt exactly like a hug against my skin.

"Go get 'em, Leslie Bear." Dad hugged me goodbye for the last time before we parted ways. "You're St. John strong, don't forget that."

"Yes, Dad." I waved back.

Mom hugged me, wiping tears from her face. "You're an absolute angel. I love you."

"I love you too!" I screamed in the same spot weeks later after I'd received the heartbreaking news. My hoodie hung in a knot around my waist, and I kept shrieking uncontrollably. Rob and Chris eventually came, but even with Rob's cigarettes and alcohol, I'd never stopped wearing that hoodie in college. It made appearances here and there, when I needed a hug, like after we lost our babies, and even a few rare, drunken times after I lost Rob and Robert Junior. But now, with the building gone, my deteriorating health, Mayor Rosewater's underhanded threat, and the struggle to stay sober, I needed a hug from my mom and dad. What I wouldn't give for the real thing. Rosewater knew I didn't even have Rob. I had a seventeen-year-old daughter as my only family.

"My company burned down, Mom," I whispered into the mirror. "And Dad, I wish you told me what really went on between you, Jeremy, and the mayor." I began to let the truth out in the mirror. I knew what he meant at the meeting before the fire. The mayor was about to come after me by using Sam to get to Candy– not Chancellor Homes–and I knew it.

The mayor's son, Jeremy Rosewater, was what came before my parents' death, not that I'd tell Trish–ever. Sam Rosewater, the mayor's brother, organized so many concerts on the east coast and had a history of making "accidents" happen. The mayor knew that I'd never be able to keep Candy away from all of the concerts unless I stopped her completely. Tears welled in my eyes as I zipped up my hoodie, trying to absorb the pain of the untold story between our families. "The mayor might kill my little girl, Mom. He might even kill me. But if I don't make it to Heaven, Mom, I never meant to be an alcoholic. It was an accident." I let the wobbly tears fall. I wanted Heaven. I just never felt deserving.

I stared at myself in the bathroom mirror and winced at the dark bags under my eyes and my singed hair that needed to be cut. I barely recognized the woman in the mirror. The bathroom smelled of the "in-case-of-emergency" strawberry scented body wash I kept under my cabinet drawer mixed with a hint of strong mouthwash. Not having an assistant or a house-keeper kept me finding things I didn't know I had and running out of things I didn't know I needed. I tugged at my dried skin on my wrist and wondered if the alleged "hydrating" wash had even worked.

Standing in the shower had been so difficult after the lung injuries, it'd worn me out. Whatever. I didn't plan for this. I hated the way the tubes looked in my nose, but then again, I hated having to rebuild what felt like my entire life. I sighed. I guessed I needed to make a grocery store run for real soap and real toothpaste. I needed to schedule a true hair appointment too, but I didn't have the energy for it. I also needed to run so many reports for work. I had to know what caused the fire. I still hadn't heard from

Susan. Had she visited the hospital when I was asleep? Had she made it out okay?

I started to run the shower again purely for the steam. The steam from the shower eased my breathing a little, and I hoped maybe I'd beat the odds and handle my lung injuries better than most. The doorbell rang, shaking me back to the present, and I hurried to let Chris in.

"Hi, Chris." I hugged him and tried to maintain a calm attitude as I invited him to the couch to sit next to me.

"My Leslie." Chris fingered my singed hair. "What have you been up to?"

I gave him a coy smile.

"You're thinking about work, I can tell." Chris gave my hoodie a knowing touch, took me by the hand and led me to the kitchen table. He tilted his head towards me as he started brewing a cup of hot tea. "You can't change what's happened. It looks like it was an accident." Chris pointed to a folder on the kitchen table. "Did you get a report from the police?" Chris continued. "They could have given you more information too."

"They're on their way over," I said. "They came during my hospital stay, but I don't remember everything they said. I blacked out at least twice."

"I think that's who just pulled up." Chris motioned to the car out the window.

I nodded and went to open the door.

"Good afternoon, Leslie Chancellor?" a tall, dark-haired cop asked.

All the feelings from when the police asked me that question almost two years ago came flooding back. Even though I knew Candy was doing homework upstairs, I wanted her next to me so I could see her. Instead, I opened the door wider. "Yes, I'm Leslie Chancellor. Please come in."

A second, younger officer who I hadn't noticed took out a pad of paper and gave me a polite nod. I welcomed them both in to talk, but they looked at Chris and remained quiet.

"Chris Schaeffer is a family friend," I explained. "Whatever update about the fire you'd like to give, you can share here."

The older officer raised his eyebrows in concern. "Ma'am, you didn't do it. Your security cam footage shows a man named Drew Carrington misusing a toaster oven around eleven thirty-eight that morning. Unfortunately, it resulted in his death."

"Death?! Drew Carrington?" I whispered the words. Candy walked in at that exact moment, jaw open.

"Scott's dad died?"

I kept my gaze on Chris. What would I say? What could I even do? Sarah lost her husband due to a toaster. A toaster at my company. My stomach sloshed around inside me, and I had no words.

"I'm so sorry," I finally stuttered, blinking at everyone in the room. "Drew Carrington was an exceptional employee, an amazing architect, and I enjoyed having him as a part of the Chancellor Homes family."

"Are you pressing charges?" the officer asked.

I shook my head. "I want to go to the funeral, and I need to talk to Sarah as soon as possible. An accident killed my husband. Sarah's whole life–" I looked down at my hands. "I'd feel like the worst boss of the century. Her husband was my employee and died on the job."

"Sarah has tons of feelings right now," Chris said before he handed me a cup of tea. "If she has any hard feelings towards you, I imagine they'll dissipate in time."

I slid the cup back and forth on the table, looking at the officers, Candy, then back to Chris. "With my track record, they'll dissipate at my funeral."

# Chapter 12: Candy

I HAD TO CALL Scott. That was why he'd been avoiding me. But part of me knew to be gentle enough to not tell him Mr. Carrington caused the fire.

Scott finally picked up on the third ring, and my heart started racing. "Hey."

"Hi, Scott?" I spoke shakily into my phone on speaker while lying flat on my bed so no one would hear. "I wanted to say I'm sorry."

Silence. I watched the seconds tick by on my phone, and I searched my brain for what to say next.

"There aren't words for this, believe me, I know."

More silence.

"But I'll be praying for you, not just a sympathy card prayer, Scott. I know the difference."

"Thanks, Candy." His voice came out hoarse, as if he'd been crying the entire time.

"Your dad was an amazing person. I'm sorry this had to be the return phone call."

"Me too."

I swiped my phone to a different app to start a food delivery to Scott. I knew he'd never ask, but I knew they needed fresh food at least. "I'll see you next Saturday?" I asked.

"Sure."

"Bye."

I hung up, flopped against my pillows, and noticed my Fruit of the Spirit journal on my nightstand. God didn't want me to bear fruit in a desert like this, right? I shouldn't have to practice that right now. I was basically excused from this challenge. It would be a miracle if I could actually keep singing. After all, didn't Scott, Mom, and I need people to be nice to us during this time, after the wake of a fire?

Love, joy, peace, patience, kindness, goodness, faithfulness, gentleness, and self-control. I stared at the words in my youth group journal again as I sat in bed the next morning, surrounded by all of my frilly pillows. Life kept getting worse and changing all around me, not the other way around. I wasn't living my best life as a singer and being a changed, blossoming flower. I wrote my feelings down in Daddy's blue travel journal, thinking Chris would probably exempt me from the Fruit of the Spirit challenge at youth group after everything that happened. I scratched my leg and tossed my pillows on the floor as I crawled out of bed.

My leg burn had left me with a heart-shaped scar on my calf. I'd never be the same person, inside or out. I got dressed thinking it was impossible to bear fruit in a dry and arid land.

My phone buzzed with a text from Nina.

**Are you okay? I heard about Scott's dad.**

**Yeah, it's awful.** I sank into my chair in front of my desk as I tapped out the letters.

**Did you talk to him?**

**Yes, he's not in a good place.** My eyes misted, thinking about how awful Scott probably felt right now.

I tossed my phone on my bed and wondered why being seventeen had to be so hard.

# Chapter 13: Candy

"**H**ONEY, DO YOU THINK you could help me freshen up?" Mom asked me late Saturday night after our movie with Chris had finished. I'd been snooping over her laptop and catching words like "resignation" and "quit" in her email and had only half -paid attention to the movie.

"What do you mean?" I dreaded hearing the answer and glanced at Chris who sat in the recliner, scrolling through channels.

"If you could stand outside while I take a shower and pick out something for me to wear, that would be great. Who knew it would be hard to wash up?" Mom tried to laugh.

"Sure." My heart beat with a sense of relief that just standing wouldn't be too bad, and I remembered how hard it had been for me to take my first shower a few days ago.

Chris got up from the chair and met us at the stairwell. "I'll make dinner."

"Sounds good, thanks." Mom attempted the stairs with me behind her, and we made it to the second floor despite it taking her unusually long.

I couldn't blame her for wanting a shower. She'd been in the hospital for almost a week, and I hadn't offered to help with a light bath. Sure, she'd cleaned up the other day and they'd bathed her during her stay in the hospital, but maybe she'd needed help? Why couldn't I think kind in advance?

I set a blush pink sweatsuit with ivory trim for Mom on the bed and waited to hear the water turn off. Mom walked out in her bathrobe, smelling of strawberries and not her usual crisp linen or other softer scents. "I'll have to call to schedule a haircut before I can go anywhere. This is a mess!" She grabbed at a brittle piece of singed hair, but smiled at me. "Maybe we can ask Sharon if she can come over and you can get more highlights. Would you like that?"

Guilt panged at me. She had a few minutes without an oxygen tank, and yet she stood there asking me if I wanted to have highlights. Was I the worst daughter?

"That sounds great, Mom."

"Perfect. We can do it before you go back to school. I'll call the salon tomorrow morning and ask if they have any cancellations or emergency appointments available." She laughed. "This bird's nest is definitely an emergency."

The smell of Chris' famous spaghetti and meatballs wafted upstairs and my stomach growled. I inched closer to the door, ready to stand and go downstairs to eat.

Mom's phone rang and she reached to answer it. Within a matter of seconds, she flushed bright red. "We're going to rebuild and carry on!"

I glanced at her, saying nothing.

"Mike's just being difficult, that's all." Mom shoved her phone in her pocket and adjusted the oxygen tubing in her nose. "But my sweet princess and I were talking about hair, right?"

"Right." I caught a glimpse of my old homeschool mom and laughed with her. I desperately wanted that mother back, so much so it hurt.

Now my phone pinged in my pocket. Chris?

**Help mom stay calm up there. She needs it.**

I tapped a thumbs up, but wondered how rough healing would be.

# Chapter 14: Leslie

S WEAT TRICKLED DOWN MY back, and I tried to find a comfortable position in bed. Memories of when we first built the office flooded my dreams. Louise, our first secretary, had gushed about the beautiful space. I designed every office on the third floor. I'd been the designer, and Rob had been the businessman. When we were new, I'd helped new families select colors from the options our contractors had given us and suggested what would look best together.

That all stopped when Rob needed me to manage and take on more of a business role. I was able to keep a few "pet projects" despite the shift. They were projects I wanted to work on with a few new couples. But Rob needed me at the office. At first it was hiring. Then it was attending meetings, then land acquisition, and before I knew it, we were running the business as a team.

I turned over onto my back, trying to keep the tubes in my nose steady. They helped a lot, but some nights they were bothersome. I reached for the remote to watch television and recalled the moment when I'd teased Rob in the empty board room, asking who'd fill the chairs I'd picked out. He'd promised me a full staff and, of course, board members. I groaned. I couldn't sleep with memories of Rob like this, memories that were destroyed by the fire.

I tried to shake those memories loose and not pay attention to the fact we shared this house, this bedroom, or this television when we worked from home on late nights. I concentrated on breathing with the new device and listened to the weatherman explain how the temperature would stay in the thirties. As if we didn't know that January usually stayed frigid.

Sharon had agreed to come by and do hair tomorrow, which meant I had to look somewhat put together by at least ten in the morning. The last time I saw myself in the mirror, I needed a complete makeover. Maybe Chris was right. I'd have to start my makeover from within and try to rest.

I slid deeper under my covers and forced my eyes shut. I tossed and turned, juggling the memories that haunted me the same way the flames did. I left the television on and let the news lull me to sleep.

# Chapter 15: Candy

"HI, SCOTT?" I HELD my phone to my ear as I sat on the edge of my bed.

"Yeah?"

"Do you mind if I stop by this afternoon?"

"For what?" He sounded as flat as my bedroom door.

"Just to, well..." I fought the lump in my throat. "I know the house isn't the same anymore, and I wanted to be there for you." A few tears fell on the throw pillow I'd been leaning on.

Now Scott's voice came across the phone, thick with emotion. "Thanks, it's fine if you stop by. We don't have to go to the funeral home until this evening anyway."

My throat tightened, and all the outrageous memory monsters I'd buried seemed to spring to life after Scott and I hung up. Mom's double funeral planning, the limo, the mahogany caskets–everything rushed to my head in one painful burst. I clutched my bedspread in my fingers so tightly it hurt, and I glanced over at the Honeybrook High hoodie slung over the chair that Scott had given me almost six months ago. Life changed so quickly, and I wanted to help Scott the way he'd helped me.

I walked downstairs to find Mom making tea in the kitchen.

"Sharon will be here any minute. We'll let her do our hair in the kitchen. I know we have hardwood upstairs, but I can't take the stairs again." Her brisk tone meant she'd been up all night. I could always tell.

Sharon arrived with all the tools necessary to make us look as though we hadn't been through a war. "Do you want a bob cut, layers, or for me to take off six inches?"

"You can take off the damaged inches, but still let it fall down my back, if that makes sense?" Mom said.

"Of course."

"And you?" Sharon fluffed my messy array of curls.

"No trim for me, but I'd like to touch up my highlights, please."

"Sure thing."

Mom's silky hair that was once waist length fell across her mid-back in a butterfly haircut. Sharon curled the ends to give it the elegant finish only Mom could obtain. I sat feeling jealous that my hair didn't quite match Mom's. I had her dark hair color, but Daddy's rogue beachy curls were highlighted a warm blond to match the cozy season. I doubted that Scott would notice my cute, fresh hair. He was grieving, and I couldn't blame him for that. I wanted to tell him I'd soon be there for him.

"Goodness, what a long day," Mom sighed after Sharon left.

"It's noon, Mom."

Mom lowered her eyes. "Of course, it's only been a long day already to me."

"Your hair looks beautiful." I touched the ends of her soft curls.

"Thank you, sweetheart, so does yours."

I reached for my purse that rested in the kitchen chair. "I'm going to visit Scott," I announced.

She nodded at me. "Okay. Don't overstay your time there. They're grieving. I plan to take a nap, so when you get home, help yourself to whatever you want for lunch or dinner or whatever time it is."

"Okay."

"Please, God, help me." My prayer felt aimless as I left for Scott's house. I didn't exactly know what I'd say or how I'd help, but I knew I needed Jesus to do it.

❖❖ · ·❖· · ❖❖

"Hey, Candy." Scott wrapped one arm around me, and I caught the pained sadness in his eyes–the same soul-twisting sadness I had almost two years ago.

"Hey."

"Come in and sit down."

We sat together in the overstuffed loveseat in awkward silence as I painfully remembered the movie night we'd had with Mr. Carrington the last time I'd been over.

"Dad thought you were a doll," Scott said, breaking the silence.

A huge lump formed in my throat.

"That's why he was okay with me giving you his promise ring, you know, the one he gave my mom?"

I glanced down at my hand. Was it even more special now? Had his mom asked for it or something?

"Do you want it back?" I searched his eyes and found the spark of love buried behind his obvious pain.

"Never," he said and took my hand.

I leaned onto his shoulder. Scott's face reddened, and I placed my ringed hand in his cool, clammy one.

"It was a blessing to know your dad."

"I never met yours, but I imagine they're getting acquainted in Heaven now."

"Yeah." I let out a long sigh. "Do you think they can see us?"

"I hope so. I hope Dad is up there still rooting for me."

"Well, if your dad is cheering for you, mine is next to him rooting for me too."

"Go, Candy!" Scott rasped.

"Go, Scott!" I echoed.

Tears threatened to fall if I said anything more, and the two of us fell into a moment of silence before Scott hugged me tighter.

"Thanks for being faithful, Candy." Scott's tear-stained face told me God heard my prayer.

# Chapter 16: Leslie

L IKE I HAD TOLD my therapist, Chris had become so special over the last few months. I didn't see my heart falling so hard. I glanced at the kitchen table, his forgotten water bottle waiting from the night before waiting for his return. I missed seeing him as I worked from home today. I wondered if he'd ever ask me to, well... my thoughts trailed off as I popped my second phone into a lavender and white striped case. I tried to work. "Good morning, this is Leslie Chancellor, am I speaking to Cody?" I waited to hear confirmation from my employee and project manager.

"This is he."

"How are you doing, Cody?" I toyed with Chris' water bottle as I sat at the table, then popped open my laptop.

"I wasn't there for the fire. I was on site for a housing project. Were you there?"

"Yes." I suppressed the irritation in my chest and skimmed the reports Susan had compiled. "I wanted to talk about repairing the Chancellor building."

The building had sustained so much damage. I didn't want to hear what I knew Cody would say.

"When do you want my demo crew out there?" Cody asked.

I paused. The words 'demo crew' officially applied to Chancellor Homes, and it knifed my heart.

"How soon can we have a team on site?" My voice threatened to give me away, but I couldn't let it.

"Next week."

"Fine. Please give me a cost estimate and a timeline. It will look the exact same as before. I have those plans with me, and I will personally supervise this project." I found my hardest professional tones to mask the pain of knocking down the building my husband promised me he'd fill with staff members and our futures. The building had seen twenty years of celebrating wins, home schooling our daughter, actually, almost giving birth to our daughter there, comforting Rob after his parents passed, and chasing our goal of homes for everyone. Gone. All of it gone.

"Yes, ma'am."

"Please make sure your team stays safe on site. We don't want any more injuries."

"Is that all, ma'am?"

"Don't throw away any furniture that can be saved and don't decorate anything."

"Yes, ma'am. Who's coming to collect those things?"

I gazed over at the living room and saw the last family photo of Rob, Candy, and me with a tiny bump that we took at the old building and swallowed hard. "I'll schedule movers to help your crew members go through and collect the salvageable before you come through with that wrecking ball of yours. I'll be on site later to see the progress."

"Sure thing."

I hung up, my heart heavy with grief. How did I lose the building in one afternoon when I was trying to keep the company afloat? I shook the stray thoughts loose and left the kitchen table to set about finishing the laundry.

Not at all work. Fixing things, restoring things, not working at all.

After the towels were folded, I dialed my payroll department.

"This is Leslie Chancellor," I said, one hand on top of the towels. "I want to make sure all of our hourly employees, including our custodians, are being paid at half salary while we rebuild." I thought of Jack trying to care for his family after a fire took his job. I kept trying to help build a community so all of my staff, including him, could afford to live in Honeybrook, but it wouldn't be helpful if I reduced everyone's income to zero.

"I'm not sure we have the budget for that," Connie told me.

"Well, move what you need to around," I said. "This is non-negotiable."

"Okay," Connie said, then hung up. With administrative staff that seemed to be so uptight, I'd have to be the one to pull everyone back into Chancellor Homes again safe and sound. I had to fix everything on my own.

My phone rang. "Leslie Chancellor."

"Ms. Leslie?" Anna's voice on the phone sounded panicked.

"Hi, honey, how are you?"

"Um, I heard about the fire and everything. I'm outside, can we talk for a moment?"

When I got to the door, Anna was chewing on a fingernail and was significantly bigger than she had been the last time I saw her. "What's wrong?" I asked.

"A friend told me you were really hurt in the fire," Anna said before she even walked inside.

"Well, yes." I motioned for her to come in. "Candy burned her leg pretty bad too, but she's healing quickly."

Anna lowered her eyes as she entered and placed one hand over her stomach. "This doesn't change anything, does it?"

I read the desperation in her face as she stood just over the threshold of the front door. She wanted a second chance in life, and I understood. Our eyes didn't meet. A second chance at a lot of things in my own life sounded amazing right now. My own teenage memories raged like a fire in my head, and I could barely think in the present.

"Everything stays the same. I'll take him or her," I said, but thought about how I never had the chance to ask Chris what he thought about it. I wondered if Michelle was making Anna's pregnancy more difficult than it had to be, and I ran my fingers through my hair. I couldn't bear to lose anything else. I was so excited to have a new baby again.

Anna breathed a sigh of relief. "I'm sorry you were hurt, but I'm so glad you'll take him."

I smiled, not catching what she said at first. When it finally registered, I felt the wind go out of me even more than normal. "Wait," I said, "it's a boy?"

Anna nodded and gave a soft smile. "Yeah."

I hugged her, thinking Chris might be excited when I told him about the possibility of a son. "He's going to be beautiful, honey, don't you worry. Trust me. Let's talk about you. What are you going to college for?"

"Nursing." Anna looked at me. "I owe Honeybrook."

*She was building guilt like me*, I thought.

"You owe nothing to Honeybrook other than being Anna Anderson," I told her. "You are enough."

Anna's eyes welled with tears and she nodded. "Thank you."

I nodded in response as she left and thought about how I'd drunk so heavily to forget anything and everything that hurt me. And in my next meeting with the mayor next week, my original pain would be glaring me in the eyes again. I wished I could pour a tall glass of anything strong enough to forget it, as my mind turned back in time. I shook my head as grief revisited me, and I waved goodbye as Anna stood at the door to leave.

"We'll keep in touch." I tried to sound encouraging as I fought the worry about my past coming to bite me. Only I knew that. Well, me and the mayor. But he had the upper hand these days. And I knew what he wanted. I went to the kitchen, popped one of my anti-anxiety pills, and hoped for the best. After all, hope was really all I had.

❧ ⸺ ◆ ⸺ ❧

"You know how to keep me smiling." I sat on the couch after the band had left for the evening and Candy had gone to finish her homework.

Chris took my hand and squeezed it softly. "I'm so glad, because I love you, Leslie."

My heart caught. After everything we'd gone through—I'd gone through— he'd hung in there through the thick of it, at least after Rob died anyway. He loved me and he'd shown it. And if I had to admit it, I loved him too. But I was suddenly Leslie Chancellor, Robert Chancellor's widow, sitting in the house we built, owner of the business we started. I'd known Rob for almost thirty years. And it had been Rob, not Chris, who'd let me stay in their dorm when I was hungover after my parents died.

"She should go home," Chris had said.

"She doesn't have a home to go to," Rob whispered, my foggy brain barely hearing him. I twisted on the couch and felt around the floor for a water bottle.

"She has grandparents."

"Who told her they'll see her for the holidays." Rob sat down next to me.

Chris' angry expression startled me as our eyes met once he sat down opposite me and Rob. "Eight times, Leslie. You've been drunk here eight times this semester."

Rob held me close. "And if you need eight more, I promise to be here. Not just your hangover guy, hopefully the guy that will always make you smile."

And Rob always had. I'd tossed that story back at Chris a few times after some rough nights he'd witnessed. I wondered if he thought I held that against him? I didn't. Chris apologized later after we learned I had severe anxiety and promised him I just needed something to stay calm. Neither Rob nor Chris encouraged my drunkenness, but we were teens. Nineteen-year-olds shouldn't have to figure out everything. But, back then, we never should have used liquor to treat pain. And now, Chris had thrown all he had into being the best friend and version of himself he could be. I loved him for him, all he did, and every memory, both good and bad.

"I'll love you forever." Chris squeezed my hand. "No matter what."

The way Chris said it stopped me. I looked into his dark, brown eyes and let myself relax for a moment. His calm, unassuming spirit was rare. And I knew in that moment, I wasn't replacing Rob. I was about to take Chris by the hand and walk into the sunset with him until we found the end of the ever-winding road called life. I nodded as I thought about new memories and new moments with a longtime friend who was turning into a fresh new love.

"Leslie?" Chris' eyes held an ounce of concern.

My heart skipped two beats. A final bittersweet moment flitted across my chest as I thought about Rob, our dreams, and our legacy. They'd never die. We had Candy and Chancellor Homes. We'd done that. Chris? I could definitely make more memories.

"I love you too." I smiled at him.

Chris leaned over and kissed me on the forehead. "You are the light of my life." He kissed me again on the cheek, softly, then my neck, and finally our lips met. It was perfect.

A fresh warmth came over me and for the first time in a long time, I felt myself blush. We'd entered that sweet more-than-dating season, even though we weren't engaged. My mind traveled to the thought of being a family of three again. Chris whispered so low in my ear, it tickled and I let myself laugh. Maybe I wouldn't need therapy if I could feel this good again. We'd be a couple, helping Candy grow into the beautiful young woman I knew she would be. And I could cradle a baby too.

The baby! I forgot to mention the baby! Chris pulled me closer, and I rested my head on his shoulder. Could I have joy again after so much loss? Chris squeezed my hand as we silently watched the weather forecast. The way he looked at me had completely changed, and I loved it. The baby? I decided it could wait. After all, this was our moment.

# Chapter 17: Candy

"**W**E'VE KNOWN CHRIS FOR a long time. Don't you think he's like family?" Mom asked me at the dinner table filled with hot deliveries from an Italian restaurant. Violet Vernon discussed Honeybrook news on the television droning on in the background, while I tried to focus on the part where Mom wanted to "be more serious" with Chris. I mean, dating was bad enough. Why press it?

"But he's not Daddy," I pushed back.

"He doesn't want to be. Think of it as him joining our team." Mom slowly pulled a piece of garlic bread apart and popped a small piece in her mouth, eyeing me the whole time. "He'd still be Chris to you, unless you ever change your mind."

"You might marry him." A wave of memories crashed across my mind of me, Mom, and Daddy doing our homeschool life, co-ops and all. Yeah, we lived a different life now, but did we have to make Chris permanent? I guess, maybe? I liked him enough, but he wasn't Daddy in the least bit.

"And what's wrong with that?" Mom sipped the coffee she shouldn't have been drinking that late.

I thought about it more as I swirled the pasta around on my plate. Chris could be an adopted uncle sort of step-dad. Kind of. Maybe. But he'd have to watch it and stay in his lane. I mean, dating was mostly harmless. So far their dating hadn't been that bad. But getting married made it... well, official. But Chris was like family already, so as long as Chris got the memo he'd never be my actual dad, I didn't have an actual problem... mostly. I didn't say any of those things out loud, though. I just smiled at Mom and said, "Nothing."

I knew I'd probably cry if they did get married. Not the tears of joy kind of crying. It would be like saying goodbye to my old life all over again.

# Chapter 18: Candy

I SAID I WANTED to be a singer, but I couldn't sing at the funeral when Mrs. Carrington had asked me. I didn't think I could sing in the same church where we'd said goodbye to Daddy. So during the graveside service, I sat in a foldout chair in the grass next to Mom and solemnly paid my respects with the dozens of others who knew Mr. Carrington. I hadn't known that Mr. Carrington had been in the military. The American flag draped over his casket, and the soldiers lined up to give him a six-gun salute. I held Scott's hand as each shot exploded from its barrel, and he squeezed my hand back. Both of us let unashamed tears roll down our faces as the smoke from the last shot faded into the air. Mine were for the fact I was back at the place my life both ended and started. Daddy's and Baby Robert's graves were next to Mr. Carrington's. The green canopy we stood under that accompanied the ritual of saying goodbye for the last time yet again tore at my heart with a pain I never expected. I cried for Mr. Carrington too. He'd been such a kind man, bringing Mom home in his car and everything while she and I were struggling a few months ago. The soldiers folded the flag and tucked the shells on the inside before they handed it to Mrs. Carrington, who sobbed audibly.

"Your father was an amazing person," Mom told Scott once the service ended. The cold air forced her to wear a scarf around her nose and mouth.

"Thank you," Scott managed.

We didn't let go of each other's hands. Mom walked with Mrs. Carrington, and we all piled into the limo. Even then, Scott and I couldn't let go. There's something about loss that pulls people together, like the way pulling on a knot only makes it tighter.

Scott needed me and I needed him.

Mrs. Carrington adjusted her tweed coat, wiped her eyes, and composed herself. I remembered the way Mom had been in so much post-surgery pain from walking after Daddy's funeral, we had to have her lie down in the backseat. Today, she was as sad as the rest of us, but at least she was able to sit up this time. Scott's eyes softened as he gently let go of my hand, and, from his moistened eyes, I could tell he'd come to the painful realization I'd arrived at a few days ago. We only had our mothers left now. I tried not to think the rising thought in my head. The thought that mine was the sickest.

The limo took us home, and only then did I let go of Scott's moist hand.

"Talk later?" I asked.

"For sure."

Mom and Mrs. Carrington exchanged hugs in the driveway, and both of them cried yet again.

Scott looked at me with damp eyes. "I understand why you wanted a song about your dad now."

My eyes stung. "Your dad will get one too."

"Thanks, Candy."

Mom couldn't handle the cold weather any longer, scarf or not. Her attempts at discreetly adjusting her scarf to support her breathing didn't go unnoticed by me or Mrs.

Carrington who made the first move to leave the drive-way.

"I'll call you later, Sarah," Mom said.

"Thank you." Mrs. Carrington got in the limo for the rest of their ride home. I moved closer to Mom and waved to Scott softly, letting the memory of his tight grip stay in my mind. We all need a hand to hold sometime, and today I was able to hold his–the day when he needed it most. I twisted the promise ring around my finger. Promises were so much deeper than I realized. It meant showing up for this kind of stuff too.

# Chapter 19: Leslie

MY STOMACH TWISTED AS I rang the doorbell of the Carrington's home. The hot casserole I held warmed my hands as I waited and thought of Sarah being a widow like me now. She had no career to fall back on. As a homemaker, she had depended on Drew for their bread and butter. Without his income, I didn't know what she planned on doing. Drew had me by at least three years, making him fifty. My head spun with the possibility of personally retiring her since we were friends or whether or not she'd be put off and think it was charity. *I need to know what her plans are,* I thought as Sarah let me inside.

"The police told me Drew started the fire." Sarah sank into the couch slowly a few minutes after I removed my coat, and I worried she'd pass out. It had only been a few days after the funeral. Stopping by with hot food I'd pre-ordered was the only thing I could think of doing to help ease some of her pain.

I sat down next to her and said, "Yes."

"Are you pressing charges?" Sarah began to play cat's cradle with her fingers.

"Sarah, he's paid the ultimate penalty already." Unexpected tears fell as I took her hand. My voice quivered. "I want my building back, the one my husband promised me, but I can never get it back now, and no amount of money can fix it. I can rebuild it, I can restore it, but I can never regain it."

"I'm sorry, Leslie."

"I'm sorry too. Your husband was an amazing person and a brilliant architect. There are no hard feelings, Sarah. Please, please understand that." I forced the words out as the stray feelings of pain bounced around in my head–the rubble from the fire, no final moments to walk around the building, and only pictures of us in the building from years ago.

Sarah pressed her lips together and nodded. The grief in the air stung me somewhere deep as a fellow widow. She and I were victims of an accident, and I could never hold her permanently responsible for her husband's mistake. I'd have to move on and rebuild my late husband's vision. And I had the house we built together to do it from.

# Chapter 20: Leslie

I T HAD BEEN TWO weeks since the fire, and it still felt like yesterday to me. In an effort to maintain control, I sat in my home office and sent out an email for the development on the property the mayor and I were fighting over.

"Let's clear the ground. I'll work out the details with Rosewater later." I messaged Mike from my new phone. After all, what was the harm in that?

I opened my laptop and clicked the app to start my video call with my development team. I worked from home, like the rest of my staff, but that only meant two hundred emails, phone calls, and video meetings. One person died, eight people resigned, and I had to interview for another personal assistant.

"When are you meeting with the mayor again?" Mike asked me on the video call.

"I had to reschedule," I said. "I haven't been well enough to have a meeting."

"Let me know when you do." Mike moved closer to his screen. "I'm happy to go with you."

"Thanks, Mike." I twisted my hair with my finger. "But I'll handle it. I've talked to old Mayor Rosewater before."

"If you change your mind and want a man with you, just let me know," Mike pressed.

I knew he hated a woman being his boss and that he wanted to fill in for every spot Rob would have done, evident by him constantly overstepping his boundaries—even in the small moments like now. He would never have Rob's place. Over my dead body. "It will be fine, thanks."

My phone rang and I immediately answered it and muted my video meeting. "Leslie Chancellor."

"Hey, the demo crew is out here and I wanted to let you know we were able to salvage some of the original furniture from the right side of the building. We filled a moving truck for you."

"Thank you, Cody," I sighed.

"I thought you'd like to know we saved Mr. Rob's picture from your office along with two of your family photos."

My heart caught, and I walked to the kitchen to keep myself from crying.

"Where did you want me to send the truck?"

"You can have it sent to my house," I said. "How far along is your team?"

"We had to knock down pretty much everything, but we can use a few of the original, undamaged bricks to build a memorial outside of the new building, if you like."

"That would be beautiful, thank you."

"You got it. The building should be back up in about six to eight months."

*Ugh,* I thought. It would be summer by the time I was back in my second home. I didn't think I could be out of the office for that long. I mean, at least I wouldn't be walking as much, but still, I missed my in-person buzz. I felt my chest tighten from the stress, and I went back to my video call.

"My apologies." I turned on my camera. "What is the development team thinking?"

Mike laughed. "We can build it!"

"What? Where?"

"Your development in New York. It's gold."

Happy tingles ran down my spine, practically electric. Even though I still had dreams for my hometown that I wouldn't give up for New York or anywhere else, I still loved the start of a new project. Candy performed in New York in two days, and I would be there too to finalize the deal. Everything was coming together again.

# Chapter 29: Candy

W E HELD BONUS PRACTICE in the deluxe studio as we prepared for the upcoming concert, but we still didn't have anyone to play the drums.

"Who's the new drummer going to be?" I asked Chris. "This is our only shot at making a good impression for Grace Unchained."

"There's a guy named Nate," Chris suggested. "He's down for performing on the spot in two days."

"Nate from the swim team?" I asked about the muscular guy who every girl except me swooned over. Nina quickly bobbed her head.

"Let's invite him over tonight!" Nina suggested.

I hid my smile.

Scott's jawline hardened and he took my hand. Competition much?

Chris answered with a smile. "I did, but he can't make it. He'll make our last practice. If he misses, Randy has a drummer in New York who can fill in too."

I nodded at Chris while stepping up to the mic with Scott.

Scott held his guitar, and I tilted my hand to let the three tiny diamonds in our promise ring glimmer. New boy in the band? No bother. He softened his shoulders, and I squeezed his hand reassuringly.

"Can't wait to meet him," he said.

I smiled. At least he got jealous. And looked cute when he did. What I wouldn't give to make a single with that guy. Or even better, to be famous together. I inhaled deeply, letting myself feel the rush of us possibly being rockstar status in a matter of days, weeks at the most. After all, this is what my heart had prayed for.

# Chapter 22: Candy

T HE LAST DAY BEFORE the concert, I had one-on-one tutoring at school for the SATs. The same SATs that would determine whether or not I'd ever perform again. The real SATs were three months away, and Max, my in-school private tutor, didn't help much. I mean, sure, I was ready for the language arts portion, but math? It seemed like a foreign language to me completely. I wished there was a way I could use music to help me remember formulas and theorems, but I hadn't come up with anything. I slouched forward on the tiny wooden desk and tried not to make eye contact with Max. Some colleges didn't even need the SATs anymore, but Mom insisted I take them so I could get into the "family college." Traditions.

"Thanks," I told him after we parted ways in the hallway to go home. I'd spent every Friday after school studying with Max, but secretly I was waiting for band practice days and youth group days. I didn't even care about the SATs, but Mom's threat loomed over me. I couldn't lose the band. I only had a few more weeks to pass the practice SAT and just a few semesters left to pass both the test and hopefully stay in the band. I scanned the Fruit of the Spirit challenge poster on the wall as I left for the day and sighed. The other day in youth group, Chris hadn't taken me aside to say anything about me being excused. He'd only told me, "Don't forget to keep adding to your journal."

I let out a breathy sigh as I walked past the fire-singed spot on the road where we lost Daddy, feeling a little salty about my whole school career. Chris really should have exempted me from the Fruit of the Spirit challenge. I had enough going on and I'd been through enough. Plus, the biggest challenge was the SATs, right? Or was it staying with the band? Or was it both? The fire had put the most unreal wrench in my life, and some days it still didn't make sense why it happened.

I inhaled a deep breath of cold, dry January air and trudged down the road. It had snowed some, and it crunched beneath my shoes as I made my way over the partially shoveled road. Scott didn't need afterschool tutoring, so he wasn't there to walk with me. Nina was too young for the SATs. Anna didn't go to school with us anymore since she became pregnant and was sent to an alternative program for pregnant youth.

I pulled my ivory puffer coat tighter as I walked the remaining few blocks to the development and wondered if I should ask for a car for my birthday. Honeybrook could be fiercely cold this time of year. As I turned toward the house, my thoughts drifted to the band. Would we perform well enough tomorrow for Grace Unchained Records to consider us? That was a test I absolutely did not want to fail. Ever.

❧ ❖ ❧

We had an amazing flight out to New York with perfect blue skies and puffy white clouds. I was used to first class treatment, but not Chris, Scott, Nina, or Nate, so it warmed my heart to see them react to the extra kind service. In the past, Mom had ordered wine with Daddy then got a spa treatment, but this flight was too short for either. However, she did try to relax and reclined her seat back to rest for most of the flight. My band members looked at me. Mom was truly asleep and I looked down. Mom spent so many days working and so many nights awake saying she couldn't sleep because of her new illness. I was happy for any sleep she was able to achieve. By the time we landed, it had only been two short hours and Mom looked confused by the somewhat rough landing.

Scott grabbed his suitcase, then mine and Chris took Mom's. Scott and I held hands as we walked into the crowded airport.

"So, we're being picked up in a limo?" I asked.

"Yes," Mom said letting out a giggle. "I thought it would be fun to do this in style."

"You have the coolest mom," Nina said and I smiled. We piled into the limo awaiting us and pulled off to go to the hotel.

The view from my window displayed beautiful chaos. New York City in all its glory looked like a dance of every creative piece of humanity clamoring to be either seen, heard, smelled, or in the case of the many restaurants, tasted. I wanted to taste the ever-popular New York style pizza, but with the awful traffic, Mom insisted on us going straight to the hotel so she could prep for her meeting.

"Ms. Susan booked our rooms for us last month before she left," Mom began, "and I'm so grateful to her for that. We have a girls' suite and a boys' suite."

I excitedly moved towards the limo door, and Mom laughed. "Wait until we park, Candy."

I shot her a smile. I wondered what else she and Mom had cooked up for this moment. I mean, tonight's winter carnival was amazing all by itself, but having my mom fully present made it twice as special.

Inside the hotel, the black marble floors and the Victorian style chandeliers gave it a regal feel. The concierge service quickly gathered all of our belongings and took us to the third floor.

"The ladies have suite B and the gentlemen have suite A," Mom continued, then handed us the plastic card keys. "Don't lose these, please." I'd lost keys before on past trips, so the request was well warranted.

Scott slipped one arm around my waist. "We perform in a few hours, what are you thinking?"

"I think this is amazing!" I let out a giggle as I opened the door to the girls' suite and placed the guitar on the couch.

Everyone followed me, and I gave a mini twirl in the middle of the kitchenette. "I'm about to sing in front of New York City!" I sang the words.

Mom laughed. "Yes, you are." She hugged me close. "I am so proud of you."

"Thanks, Mom." I returned the hug and glanced at Scott. He had been talking to Nate since we got to the plane. Nate seemed quiet, yet friendly. Nina approached me and Mom.

"So, there's multiple bedrooms in this suite?" I asked.

"Yes, honey," Mom answered. "Everyone has a bedroom, but we'll share the kitchen and this tiny living room. And the same goes for the guys' room." Mom kept one arm wrapped around me as she spoke. "I think we need to have a spa day later, ladies, while we're here and the guys–" Mom stopped to laugh. "Whatever makes you happy, have fun doing that."

Chris laughed too. "We're going to catch a movie when Ms. Leslie comes back for the girls. How does that sound?"

Scott and Nate nodded their approval.

"Where are you going now?" I asked Mom.

"I have a short back massage, then a meeting, honey," Mom whispered in my ear, as if she wanted to reassure me of something. Mom always got massages when traveling, and Daddy had always made sure she had as many as she needed during the trip. For some of our family work-cations that ended up being every day, depending on how long and how intense the business was going to be.

The guys left to go to their rooms, and Mom, Nina and I started unpacking. I had the room across from Mom, and Nina had the room next to mine. Just as I put my glitter makeup bag in the bathroom, Nina bounced in.

"Hey, Candy, do you think your mom would be okay if we walked around before dinner and explored?"

I stopped arranging my hair products in the bathroom to think about it. My overly anxious mom would probably choke me for even asking.

"Mom?" I called.

"What is it?" Mom walked over to my room, curling iron in one hand and a jacket in the other.

"Can Nina and I walk around while you're out?"

Mom let out a long sigh. "That would defeat the purpose of the massage, if I knew you were out in the middle of this concrete jungle. Why don't you guys explore the hotel? There's a pool, three different stores, a café, and–" She paused and reached for her phone. "I can't remember everything, but I'd feel better if the two of you were in here and not in the streets of New York City alone, okay?"

I tried not to roll my eyes. I was in high school now, which, everyone knows, is the next-to-last step before becoming an adult. So, why couldn't she treat me like one? I could be responsible. She just kept holding me back.

Mom must have caught my frustration. Her jacket brushed my hair as she whispered in my ear. "Do it for me, okay?"

Nina and I shared expressions. "So, did you want to explore the hotel?" I asked her.

She quietly nodded.

A knock sounded at the door and all three of us went to answer it. It was someone from the hotel.

"The taxi is ready for you, Ms. Leslie."

"Thanks." Mom tossed the curling iron aimlessly into her room, pulled on her coat, and gave us a quick wave goodbye. "I'll see you girls at the concert if the meeting runs long," she said.

"Okay." We followed her out the door into the long hallway in search of a gift shop. Mom turned left and got onto the elevator.

Nina laughed. "How big is this place, and where is this gift shop?"

Chris met us in the hallway with Scott and Nate. "Huge." He laughed and the corners of his eyes crinkled some. "And we're meeting in their Conference Room A, not the gift shop. Since we haven't had a chance to practice with Nate yet, I want us all to practice once before the show. We're going to arrive early to the carnival to do a sound check, too."

Nina tossed me a tiny smile. We followed the guys to the room that had been rented for us to practice. Performances had been held in this space, so the acoustics were great. But as I practiced, I felt more and more nervous. Tonight was the big performance and hopefully my chance to get the prayed-for single.

**Chapter 23: Leslie**

The doctors had told me not to travel for at least three months, and now, walking down the long stretch of sidewalk, post-massage, I understood why. I was winded, despite my oxygen and my alleged "circulation boosting" massage. I glanced at the writing on the glass door and pushed it open. The clicking of my heels alerted the secretary I'd entered the building. I smiled at her, hoping she wouldn't judge me as a former "smoker" who "made bad choices" just because I now had obvious breathing support. Maybe I did smoke, but I had been trapped in a fire too. No one here knew that. I wanted to pull the tubes out for the meeting, but I gripped my briefcase tighter instead as I followed the secretary down the hallway to the boardroom.

"Are you okay?" she asked, and I realized that my breathing had started to sound noisy again.

"Water would be great, thanks." I tried to maintain my cool as I took a seat and popped open my laptop across from a short, round old man wearing a tweed suit.

"Leslie Chancellor, nice to meet you." I shook his hand.

"McDonell, Paul." His voice came out shaky, and he sounded like Piglet from Winne-the-Pooh. "I hear you're one of the biggest names this side of the Mississippi."

I let out a warm laugh. "That was three years ago, but thank you." I thought about how proud Rob had been to win the best home builder of the year award and how much he had wanted to win it again. I scanned the documents Paul placed in front of me.

I shifted in my seat in the unfamiliar boardroom with paneled walls. The secretary came back with water and started taking notes while I put Mike on video chat. A lawyer came into the room and sat across from me. The chilly air smelled of mothballs.

"So, let's talk numbers," I began, even as I shivered a little. I knew proper etiquette called for me to remove my coat, but I didn't want to. Still, I did, letting my navy blazer remain my only shield against the uncomfortable temperature of the room. I looked over my glasses at Paul. "I think the land is only worth forty million, not the seventy-five million dollar asking price."

"Why?" Paul raised his voice, astonished. "Land is land."

I removed my glasses and met his gaze. "The water sample here came back somewhat contaminated," I told him. "We'd have to install water treatment filters in every one of our units which is a costly setback for us."

The man swiped at his nose and reached across the table. Taking my hands into his, he blinked at me anxiously. "Ms. Chancellor, forty million dollars is a good offer, but this is family land. I have two other siblings. Can't you make it sixty so we can split it evenly? Twenty million each?" He squeaked, sniffed, then leaned back. I hated emotional sales, and I didn't have time for one after the sinkhole incident.

"I could do thirty million," I retorted. "That would be even, too. It's not just the contaminated water, you know. People are aware the eastern seaboard gets coastal flooding and hurricanes. I have to factor all of those things when acquiring new property."

My phone buzzed. "Excuse me." It was Candy with directions to the concert.

**Just in case you're not in the limo with us.** She sent a smiley face.

I smiled at my phone. **Thanks.** I texted her back and slid my phone into my purse.

"Did you want more time to think about this?" I asked the man.

"Are you sure you can't go higher?"

I let out a long sigh. I always seemed stuck with family land purchases. Maxwell Homes, my competitor on this property, could offer him sixty in this market.

"The land isn't worth seventy-five" Mike said over video chat and his voice came out choppy, "We understand it's special to you, but it's not worth that much."

I glanced across the table at the lawyer. I didn't want to hurt the family.

"Tell you what. I can do forty-five million, and everyone will get fifteen million as inheritance. How's that?"

The man brightened and he turned pink. "Why didn't I think of that?"

I refrained from rolling my eyes.

"I can handle the paperwork from here," the lawyer said as he gathered up his papers.

"Perfect. Please send it to me as soon as possible so my team can look at it. We'll have surveyors on the property before the land is officially purchased, so please don't chase away any visitors." I smiled at him. "If everything checks out, I'll countersign the agreement and we'll be good to go."

"Thank you." The man stood up and shook my hand heartily.

I felt grateful for the exclusive apartments I would build, but they weren't affordable single-family homes like Rob wanted. And they were most certainly not in Honeybrook. I grabbed my purse and left, glad I'd beat Maxwell Homes to the deal.

The way out of the building seemed longer than when I walked in, but I didn't really care. I planned on grabbing coffee, finding a taxi, and heading back to my daughter who had thought I would actually be late enough to miss her concert. My phone buzzed with an email, and I reached for it again. Mayor Rosewater. Meeting Invitation. I let out a sigh and scanned the date. It was only two weeks from now, and I had to prove to him I wasn't letting Rob's dreams die. Only this time, I wouldn't have my staff anywhere near me. It would be like I was eighteen again–alone. His fake condolences after the boating accident rippled through my brain. I forced myself into the present, or at least my lungs did, as I felt them burn as I tried to get to my taxi.

"Nearest Starbucks, then the Blue Star Hotel," I told him.

I needed to be ready for Candy's sweet out-of-state debut in a few hours. I was determined to make it memorable, at least with a manicure and special hairstyle. After all, these were the precious moments I lived for.

# Chapter 24: Candy

SCOTT, NINA, AND I were singing in the conference room while Chris practiced with Nate when Mom blew into the hotel. She found us and said, "Manicures are on me, so let's go."

"I'll see you, Scott." I gave him a hug and he hugged me back, leaving me feeling so warm, I almost wanted to skip the manicure entirely.

Mom escorted us into the nail salon inside the ritzy hotel. "Your appearance on stage matters." She held onto the door and gave me a small eye roll.

We were immediately waited on by several nail artists who showed us hundreds of nail colors. I couldn't decide on one. They were all pretty, but at the same time, I didn't really know which shade would look best on me. In middle school, I had worn yellow nail polish once, but that totally didn't become me. And I'd have to wait until I got a summer tan to try for the tangerine color. I bit my lip as the nail technician waited for me to decide. "Could I do light pink with a flower design on my thumb?" I asked.

"Good idea." Her almond shaped eyes smiled at me and she set my hand in a tub of warm water. Mom must have reserved the appointment, because while Nina and I were getting manicures, she got a mani-pedi.

"What color did you pick?" Nina asked me.

"Pink, what about you?"

"Blue, only because January feels like, if it had a color, it would be blue, for the bluejays and stuff."

"I should have thought of that." I watched as the lady brushed pink on my fingernails. "Your shade of blue is a pretty color too."

My nails came out looking pretty stunning, if I did say so myself. I had a winter flower on my thumb with a gem for the center. She also gave me a glitter party nail on my pinky, so I felt pretty fancy when she finished.

Nina and I went to check on Mom, who stood with her purse open at the front desk. She'd been waited on by two technicians and was tipping everyone.

"Your mom fell asleep in spa chair," one of them told me, then laughed.

I didn't think it was funny. She couldn't sleep well at night with her condition, but they didn't know that.

"Next time, I'll try to stay awake." Mom seemed unfazed. "I need to come back."

I glanced at her lavender gel set and her matching toenails that were still drying in the complimentary foam flip flops.

"Ready, girls? We still have to do hair and makeup."

"Ready." I smiled at her and took in the fact she looked exhausted. "Did your meeting go well?"

"Yeah." She hugged me as we got on the elevator. "Chancellor Homes for the win again. We beat Maxwell Homes to the land deal, and we should break ground in March."

"Congratulations!" I admired my mom's business savvy, even if I didn't want to be a part of it myself.

"Thank you, sweetie." Mom ushered us off the elevator. "Now, for your lipstick. I want you to go dark tonight, okay? And try to use some shimmer on your eyes?"

"Can you help us pick the right shade?" Nina asked as we entered the hotel room.

Wrong question. Mom was more than happy to "help," but it took so much out of her. We sat on the couch in front of the television, allowing her to do her design magic.

She braided Nina's hair and let her borrow one of her hair combs. Then she arranged my curls and set them with hair spray.

Mom gave my curls a slightly aggressive fluff. "What are you wearing tonight?"

"Umm..." I tried to think about what I'd packed. "I think it's a denim dress?"

"Oh, honestly, Candy, it's going to be freezing." Mom folded her arms and her expression turned worried.

"Can't I wear a jacket?"

"Not when you're the performer." Mom frowned as she started tapping away at her phone.

"You'll need some layers beneath your clothes. I'm having a nearby store deliver them in an hour. Thank goodness you can fit a small, or at least, you will tonight."

"Thanks." I checked my phone for messages from Scott, but he hadn't said anything. Maybe they were still in the movie. We started to do make-up, but stopped when Mom dropped the hairbrush she'd been using on Nina's hair and started sneezing.

"Are you okay?" Nina asked, picking it up.

"I'm good," Mom said, almost sneezing again. "It's just the dust in the room." She handed us her makeup kit.

We went to the bathroom to apply our makeup, under Mom's direction of how our eyebrows, lips, and eyeshadow should look. She kept turning away to sneeze, and Nina gave me a look in the mirror.

"I'm going to grab some water." Mom left, and Nina and I were left alone to make minor modifications to our makeup.

"Pass me the mascara," I whispered.

"Your mom is so sweet," Nina said. "She sounds sick, though. Did you guys have colds last week?"

"No." I tapped my deep red lipstick a little. "We've been fine. Mom sounds a little raspy now, that's all."

Mom reentered. "You two are dolls." She wiped a makeup smudge away from my eyebrow. "I can't wait to see you both in concert tonight." All three of us looked in the mirror and we began to laugh. We really had hours before showtime!

"Thanks, Mom." I hugged her. I loved the way Mom had helped me look pretty. I felt like a cowgirl princess and was ready to go onstage and be discovered by Grace Unchained.

"Set your face." She winked at me and handed me a bottle of makeup setting spritzer. "No smudges."

I laughed and gave my face a light spray. Mom's phone buzzed and she clicked it. Nina and I paused as we heard her mumbling the email out loud. "Girls, let me tell you, never pass up the chance to sparkle. Maxwell Homes dropped their bid on land in Maryland after I closed on the property deal this afternoon. Now, Chancellor Homes can pick up land in Maryland and Virginia, making us one of the biggest home developers on the east coast. I'm going to go handle this and message my team. You two get ready to shine on stage, okay?"

<hr/>

I found Mom ten minutes later in her guest room, on the bed and drinking water.

"Sorry I disappeared for so long." She leaned back on the bed. "Mike and Wendy liked the acquisition idea I found in Maryland, but we are waiting to hear back from finance." She flipped her hair to one side and let it fall past her shoulders. "We just have to stay in the green."

*Stay in the green.* I remembered I had to tell her about how the SAT practice was still hard for me when we finished the performance. I wasn't looking forward to it at all.

"I'm going to take a nap before the concert. Stay on the lookout for a delivery person and make sure to put on your layers when you get dressed, okay?"

"I will." I felt sorry for her as she pulled the quilt closer to her and closed her eyes. It had been a long day for her. Mom usually worked from seven to one at the latest and came home to either pulmonary rehab, to go for a short walk, or to rest. It was almost four and she'd been in meetings all day, with her only break being the mini massage and mani-pedi. I closed the door softly and set an alarm on my phone to wake her in time for the concert. I hummed our lyrics in pure excitement as we finished our makeup. I had hours before I was under the limelight.

# Chapter 25: Leslie

A T THE OUTDOOR CONCERT venue, I zipped up my coat as I watched from backstage, just behind the curtain. Candy's denim dress danced in the wind. Thankfully, it didn't fly up or anything like that. Her pink boots were adorable, and they matched her nails perfectly. She sang so clearly and strongly, I thought Honeybrook could still hear her.

I have a new house being built/
It's not quite ready yet/
I hope you'll stop by and see it sometime.
It's one of a kind, one of the best/
Proof that love has stood the test/
That my soul can finally rest/
In God's country.
Heaven my final home/
The place my heart belongs/
In God's country.

"I've lost a lot and won a lot, too," Candy said to the audience. "I lost my dad, lost my baby brother, and recently my family lost our building in a fire, but what I've never lost is the love of God which is in Jesus Christ, our Lord. And if you believe that tonight, sing the rest with me."

My eyes watered as she guided the crowd into worship. Everyone around me seemed to be in a state of calm, reverent praise, but I couldn't seem to join. And for the first time, it scared me. Candy was a true believer, a faithful follower, and Heaven would be her home.

I stood, holding hands with Chris as Candy's strong voice pierced the night.

"On Daddy's headstone, there's two inches of space between the year he was born and the year he died," Candy said, catching me off guard. "But, within those two inches were a lot of years that made a world of difference. And the most important decision Daddy ever made was to accept Jesus as His Lord and Savior. So, I know the room Jesus has prepared for him looks amazing. He's working on mine, and yours, too."

My heart skipped a beat. She brought the heart of country music to New York in a pint-sized package, but why hadn't I done the simple thing she just said? That God had said? I wanted to see Rob again and the babies. And God knew I wanted Someone else to design a room besides me. The crowd cheered for her, and some people moved closer, touching the short, metal crowd control railing, breaking my thoughts as I worried they'd approach Candy. I moved to step onstage after the song finished, but Chris pulled me back.

"Leslie, she's fine. Security is at the bottom of the stage."

*Did I not commit my life to the Lord because of what happened when I was a teen? I didn't feel like God saw me then, and I'm not sure He sees me now.* I wondered why I was even thinking so deeply and whipped out my phone to try to regain control.

"Well, I still need pictures." I pressed forward a little and started snapping photos and recording a few special moments. Snow began to fall, making my phone screen somewhat drippy, but I recorded it anyway. The night sky was otherwise clear, and everyone's attention hinged on Candy's bluegrass tunes. Someone working the venue shoved in between me and Chris, and my initial fears for Candy's safety were reignited. I leaned against him a little to prevent any more strangers from passing through. "No one can protect Candy the way I can."

"Thank you, New York!" Candy shouted into the crowd. She turned, gave me a smile, then walked to the front of the stage with Scott, Nate, and Nina to take a bow. I moved out of the way as the larger band, *We the Guilty*, got ready to get on stage. There were too many people, and I didn't like backstage much. Everyone kept pushing, rushing, and talking to each other at a record speed. A tall, slim man in black wearing a headset bumped into me for the second time that night. I thought about the mayor's underhanded "suggestion" before the fire, and my heart almost stopped. I didn't know if I could do this. Chris squeezed my hand, and I gave it a firm squeeze back. I knew security was protecting Candy and her friends and concerts were like this. Something just felt off. Candy had performed before, but tonight in New York, I couldn't shake the uneasy feeling that kept skipping around inside me. I tapped my foot, even though Candy had finished singing, and glanced around for what could be causing my complete agitation. Chris placed two hands on my shoulders.

"This is just Candy's biggest performance so far, Les'. It'll get easier, I'm sure."

I sighed, thinking of all the performances in the future that I might have to stand backstage for, if she were to become popular. I pushed the notion of Sam Rosewater and the mayor's threats to the back of my head, closed my eyes, and willed myself to relax. Just as I let my shoulders down, the sound of several shots went off.

# Chapter 26: Candy

THE FIREWORKS ABOVE ME caught me off guard and Scott gripped my hand. "You're used to fireworks, right?" he teased.

"Of course," I teased back. "We do them all the time." I stared up at the sky as it exploded in red that represented the Blood that was shed because all of us are guilty and we need Jesus, our Savior. When the last red sparkles had died away, the four of us turned to walk offstage. But before we had gotten halfway off, *We the Guilty* stopped us.

Their lead singer, Grayson Lee, motioned for me to go back to the mic. "Let's give it up for these guys! *The Chosen Band* showed up and out for Jesus today!"

The crowd roared and my heart touched the stars. *Thank You, Jesus*, I inwardly prayed.

"We want to hear more of these teens who are letting God work in their lives. As a matter of fact, why don't we do another song together right now?"

I almost choked. Grayson. Lee. Sing with *We the Guilty*? Grayson Lee's eyes beckoned me to make the leap. *You've got this*, I told myself. *This is the dream.*

Mic in hand, I followed his lead. We stood next to each other, but Scott and *We the Guilty* backup singers helped form the legendary semi-circle that belonged to country singers only. I lowered my head as the words to *Amazing*

*Grace* rolled off my lips and into the freezing January air. My cowgirl hat blocked most of the chill, but my loose curls still danced in the wind as I strummed my guitar alongside Grayson Lee. Scott wore a huge grin, and I could tell he was stoked too. I saw the flashes of phones in the audience.

"Yeah!" Grayson Lee ended the song, and I added a playful riff on my guitar. He started laughing and lifted my hand in front of the New York audience. "I don't know if someone from Grace Unchained is in the audience, but someone needs to give this little lady a single."

My hands flew to my mouth and the crowd applauded.

"Thank you!" I managed to say.

"Thank God," Grayson Lee answered, "for your gift."

My heart melted as more fireworks went off. Scott, Nate, Nina, and I beamed and waved while walking offstage to find Chris and Mom, who were smiling at us with excitement too.

"Way to go, guys!" Chris hugged me and Nina and fist bumped Scott.

"Praise God!" I said. "This was the best day of the new year so far."

"Yeah," Nina answered. "I mean, who would have thought we wouldn't just open for *We the Guilty*, but also perform with Grayson Lee?"

My entire body tingled with excitement and joy. I heard more explosions and more fireworks. Everyone cheered for us. We only got to open one more night and hoped Grace Unchained would say 'yes.' Offstage, I caught the fear in Mom's eyes. She wasn't ruining this. I looked away and back out at the crowd. I loved her, but she couldn't.

# Chapter 27: Candy

I BOLTED UPRIGHT IN bed as I heard Mom screaming across the hall that night.

"Fire!" Mom screamed.

I met Nina in the hallway and glanced both ways, in search of flames, but found none.

"Mom has nightmares," I explained and gave Nina a quick shrug, but knocked on Mom's door to check on her.

"Candy?" Mom called from the other side of the wooden door.

"Are you okay?"

I heard shuffling, followed by a thud. The door cracked open, and Mom poked her head out, looking exhausted and dripping with sweat. "I'm sorry I woke you up. I guess there isn't a fire." Mom walked out into the living space and sank on the couch. "Only in my head."

I caught a quiet nod from Nina as she padded back to her room, and I gave her a weak smile.

I sat down next to Mom and she pulled me closer to her. "You should go back to bed. I'm not going to sleep tonight."

I took in the sight of my mom, her hair limp around her face and her eyes red. "I'm staying up with you," I declared.

Mom opened her mouth as if she were about to protest the idea, but then hugged me and ran her fingers through my hair softly. "You're my forever, you know?"

I nodded. "I love you too."

"If we're staying up, why don't we order room service? Would you like milk and cookies?" Mom took on her girlish grin.

I gave her a small smile. This was my mom, sober but panicked. For now, she was okay.

"Let me call and order." Mom scurried around the room for her purse. "Ordering at this hour demands a high tip." She fished around for cash.

Room service came relatively quickly, and I stood next to Mom at the door while she took the enormous oatmeal cookies and milk.

"Thank you so much," the guy said, then wiped his nose with the back of his hand. "You don't know how much I needed this." His voice came out stuffy.

"My pleasure." Mom gave his hand a small shake. "I'm glad it turned out to be the right thing at the right time."

"Yeah." The guy folded the tip in his hands then left. The door closed slowly, and I listened to the sound of his cart rolling down the hall followed by a quick sneeze.

"Is Nina asleep?" Mom asked. "We don't want to count her out."

I pranced towards Nina's room in my socks and saw the light was out. She'd been able to return to dreamland.

"Nina's sleeping."

"Well, I guess it's time to show you my college trick." Mom smiled at me. "Back in college, when I didn't have homemade cookies from your great-grandmother, I put my cookies in the microwave to make them seem like they were warm and fresh." Mom held out the plate.

I'd heard about the hack before, but I'd never really tried it. I never had the chance to. But here, with my mom in the tiny kitchenette, I was ready to taste something new. The microwave hummed as the cooled bakery cookies softened. In a matter of seconds, the timer went off and Mom used a paper towel to hand me a hot oatmeal cookie. It practically fell apart in my hands.

She bit first. "These are amazing."

"I love this hack," I agreed, as we both left the kitchenette and went back to the couch. We ate the cookies and sipped the cold milk, then turned on the television to watch reruns of old shows. I leaned against Mom's shoulder as the end credits to *Little House on the Prairie* rolled off the screen.

Mom turned and started coughing into her paper towel. She crumpled her towel in her hands. "I'm going to go ahead and take my meds now. It's practically sunrise."

I glanced at the clock on the stove. Five forty-five. We'd have breakfast with the team soon. And somehow, I wasn't tired. Maybe I'd crash later. I observed Mom taking all her medication and let my mind wander to tonight's concert. Tonight we would be opening for *We the Guilty* with our original song instead of a cover. And if it went well, this one night would hopefully send us to the big time. A single. An invitation to sing in the country music concert in Virginia. Maybe even a record. I chewed my lip as my mind soared with dreams. I hoped I'd sound good enough for Grace Unchained to say 'yes.'

Around seven, Nina bounced out of her room.

"You guys never went back to sleep?" She looked surprised.

"No." I let a soft smile cross my lips. "Mom and I had a girls' night."

"Maybe next time you can join us?" Mom placed a hand on Nina's back. "They're random, unpredictable, and usually between the hours of one and three in the morning."

Nina laughed. "Maybe."

Mom's phone buzzed and she answered it on speaker. "Leslie Chancellor."

"You're traveling, Leslie?" I heard the distinct voice of Mom's doctor. "Your voice message from last night says you felt out of breath."

Mom gave me a quick look. "I sent a message to your office after a meeting."

"You'll need to increase your oxygen," the doctor said with an audible sigh. "And try to take care of yourself."" Doctor, I'm a working mother," Mom said, glancing at the ceiling.

"All the more reason to take it slow."

I caught Mom's eyes watering after she hung up. "I hope this increase is temporary." She briskly removed her fluffy robe. "Okay, enough of that. The guys are going to beat us to the breakfast table. Let's get ready. I have a meeting in two hours, so I'm going to get changed." Mom started to twist her hair up as she spoke. "And you girls need to get dressed for the day."

I nodded and went to my room to pick the sweater and jeans I planned to wear before the concert. We had a huge day ahead of us, or at least a big night.

# Chapter 28: Candy

W E SMASHED THE CONCERT that night. And Mom didn't go into panic mode. Grace Unchained would have to sign us on after a performance like that, right?

"Way to go," Grayson Lee told me as I walked offstage with my team. "Don't let anything stop you, Candy."

*We the Guilty* got on stage and I listened, letting his words sink into my heart. A fresh, roaring surge from the crowd filled me, and my brain spun with excitement as I soaked in the feeling of being that much closer to my dream of being a famous singer. After the concert, we signed a few autograph books and shook a lot of hands. Chris kept us moving since we were behind schedule to catch our flight back to Philly. I snapped as many pictures as I could for social media and followed the team back out into the cool night air. Being in the limelight for a little bit brought so much joy, I never wanted to leave it behind. I'd tasted my dream and now I wanted to keep it going forever.

Mom awaited us in the car.

"You guys did an amazing job! Thank goodness you're safe."

"Thanks!" I hugged her and slid into the seat next to her. "So?"

"So, we'll get your SAT scores, I'll see the next concert in Virginia if it goes through, and make my final decision." She shook her head at me. "Persistent, aren't you?" She gave me a tight hug.

Nina and Nate sat across from me and Scott in the limo. Chris slid next to Mom, shut the door, and we headed off for the airport. Weird how I had to go from singing at this weekend's Winter Carnival concert to being back at Honeybrook High in about five more days, studying for the SATs.

Mom gifted us first-class seating for the return flight too, and Nina gave Mom a quick hug as a thanks.

The flight from New York to Philly came with more turbulence than expected. Chris looked concerned and switched seats with Mom to protect her head from the window as the plane gave us a hard jostle. Scott held my hand the entire time, while Nina kept reading required books from school and sharing them with Nate. Were they... crushing? A soft smile came over me as I thought about sweet, quiet Nina.

"God gave you the most amazing voice," Scott whispered in my ear, and I immediately turned my attention to him.

"And He gave me an amazing guitarist to sing with," I whispered back. I got all the cozy tingles as he leaned in closer and squeezed my hand a little tighter. The miracle of the night was that I could still sing despite having so much Scott Carrington on the brain. I mean, were we ever apart? I never wanted to be. Weird how I survived a fire, but teetered between "in love with Scott" and "cause of death: Scott Carrington's eyes melted her heart and she couldn't breathe." Did anyone else ever feel like this? This crazy, mixed-up floaty feeling? I smiled back at Scott and his cheek dimpled.

As we descended, the turbulence seemed to increase even more before we hit the runway. I noticed Mom looked green as we landed in the rain. She must have said something, but I couldn't make it out, and Chris grabbed her suitcase quickly.

A limo awaited us outside the terminal to drive us the last three hours home to Honeybrook. The flight attendants and Chris helped Mom off, and we quickly followed with our luggage. We were hot and cramped inside the smaller limo than last time, but we managed.

The icy air had triggered Mom's cough, which sounded painful.

"Here's a cough drop." Chris offered Mom one, but she waved it away.

"That won't work. I need my inhaler." Mom rummaged around in her purse until she found the tiny device. It suppressed the cough for a bit, but she seemed worn out from traveling anyway. She fell asleep on Chris' shoulder, and Chris gave us a serious expression to not wake Mom or say anything teasing.

Scott and I snapped selfies for social media, and I posted them as we drove along the stretch of highway, praying we'd be invited to the next country music concert in Virginia. I texted Mom's photos of me to myself and posted the concert photos as well as the travel photos. I glanced out the window at the bridge we were about to cross. The traffic had come to a full halt and we were surrounded by cars on both sides. All I could see were headlights and more highway after the bridge. I glanced as Mom shifted positions in her sleep across from me. Silent tears ran down her face, and Chris did his best to just let them fall on his shirt. It was this sort of moment that worried me. My panic-stricken mom would ruin future concerts and destroy my dream before it even became a reality.

Scott and Nina texted me in our group chat.

**Prayers for Grace Unchained offer.**

I read Scott's message then looked up at him.

**I hope so.** I texted back.

**We sang with Grayson Lee!!!!** Nina added and the three of us exchanged smiles.

Mom emitted a soft sob, and I glanced at Chris. Would he help her?

"Leslie," Chris whispered.

Mom snapped awake, looking confused. "What's wrong?"

"Is there something you need?" Chris asked.

Mom gave me a panicked look.

I mouthed the words, "You were crying."

"Um, I'm fine." Mom caught the cue. "I'm sorry I fell asleep on you."

Chris didn't seem convinced and handed Mom a bottle of water. "We only have two more hours before we're back in Honeybrook."

"We should have eaten dinner," Mom announced. "This was the longest way back ever."

"Did you want to stop?" I asked.

"It's up to you kids," Mom said. "It's past midnight."

Scott and I looked at each other. Food sounded amazing. And just ten minutes after we agreed to stop, a small-town diner in West Virginia shone in front of us. After burgers and greasy fries, we rolled back into Honeybrook, suitcases full of dirty clothes but plenty of warm memories. In the driveway, my phone pinged with notifications from more than one social media platform. "Christian Teen Band Turns Carnival into Church." I read someone else's post. It had thousands of likes. "Christian Kid Singers go Viral After Singing with Grayson Lee." I looked down at the like count. That post was viral. I saw it eight more times and showed it to Scott, who went from almost-asleep to astounded within seconds. He took the phone from me.

"For real?" he asked.

I nodded. "They really liked us."

Scott hugged me, then we passed the phone to Nate and Nina who were equally excited. Chris and Mom were asleep, but we'd catch them up later. We were home now anyway.

Scott stood with me in my driveway as Chris got Mom into the house. "Call you tomorrow?"

"Absolutely," I said as I twirled my suitcase a little before rolling it up to the door.

"You kids did an amazing job," Chris said once he returned to grab Mom's bags. "I'll give y'all a ride home as soon as I make sure Ms. Leslie and Candy are safe inside."

I waved at Scott and Nina before heading in. I was so excited about basically becoming an overnight sensation, since our impromptu song with We the Guilty sparked a ton of social media posts about us– posts I'd shared, reposted, and that thousands of people had shared. We were trending, and I knew I wouldn't sleep. Mom, however, plopped her purse next to the door, gave Chris a hug, and immediately fell asleep on the couch without saying one more word. Before turning off the lights and heading up myself, I noticed more tears were racing down her face.

❖❭❭ ·· ◆ ·· ❬❬❖

The next morning, I tried to unpack, hoping that when Mom felt better, she'd feel better about another performance. I scrolled through the pictures on my phone with me, Nate, Nina, and Scott. Nate seemed like he would be a really nice addition to the band. I grabbed all my dirty clothes and dumped them in the hamper. I wished I could have gotten to know Nate a little better. We'd all just been so focused on playing the song instead of connecting, something I knew I struggled with sometimes. I kept scrolling through the pictures a second time. Nina and Nate? I was right. But then I remembered Nina sharing her books and wondered. I hadn't connected with Nate, but maybe something was going on. Nate winked at Nina in one of those shots. What did I miss? I turned on my music streaming app and let the events replay in my head. When could Nate and Nina have had a moment? I mean Scott and I had some sweet moments too, though. I reached for the hair tie on my desk and pulled my curls into a ponytail. Either way, I was grateful the concert had gone well. Daddy would have been proud. I hoped Grace Unchained would call us. I hoped so much, it almost hurt.

I heard Mom talking downstairs, and I wondered who came over. I paused midway down the stairs when I saw her alone at the table with a glass of milk.

"I'm scared." Mom started crying. "If they offer her a single, she could get hurt. God, I love her. But You know the Rosewaters. I know the Mayor won't stop. He'll make it look like another accident. Please don't–" Mom started crying harder and I looked down, tempted to walk back upstairs. "I guess I've got no real right to pray, since I'm not an official Christian." She sniffled. "And I don't even know if I've ever done it right." Her voice wobbled and a lump formed in my throat. "But please don't take my last daughter. Please. Amen."

And there, standing on the stairs, it felt like a wooden door had slammed on my face. I wanted a healthy mom, but I wanted a life onstage too. Would she always be a nervous wreck? Would God tell me 'no', as the answer to my prayer and tell Mom 'yes' because she was more desperate, sicker, and hurting? I let out a huff of frustration and hurried away, wondering if I could make a single to prove my faith in God toward Mom despite all odds.

# Chapter 29: Leslie

"LESLIE, SHOULD WE CALL a friend for you?" The older woman who led our Alcoholics Anonymous meetings sat down on the cold floor next to me. I hadn't been able to move after the meeting. Everyone had left and I faced red, empty chairs and one huge window. More tears escaped me and the urge for a strong drink and smoke kept tugging at me.

"I lost my building in a fire. My medication isn't working." I let the ugly tears fall. "My lungs are so damaged, but I have to keep up with my rising star of a country singer daughter. I have to keep her safe." I pressed my hand over my middle as the beautiful side effects of said "stronger dose" wreaked havoc on my stomach.

The older woman turned to face me, brushed my hair back, and stared straight into my eyes. She leaned against the beige wall and took my hand into her jewelry laden one. "You've come further than you think," she said. "Remember what we say at the beginning of our meetings?"

"Grant me serenity..." I choked out the words. "...to accept the things I cannot change."

Her eyes softened and she nodded. "I can't change your health or undo the fire. But I can encourage you to take care of yourself moving forward and to focus on restoring your building."

I lowered my head and clicked my nails together softly. "My daughter is so young."

"All the more reason to try to stay healthy for her. You're fifty-two days clean, Leslie. That's something to be proud of. You can make it to sixty."

I turned to cough, and I knew my lungs couldn't take any more abuse from smoking. Standing slowly, I wiped the remaining tears from my eyes and squeezed the older woman's hand. "Thank you," I said.

"No problem." She stood and hugged me. "Incidentally, I struggled with the same thing after I lost my son and my husband divorced me. Trust me, you don't want to go back."

I chewed my lip to prevent further tears.

"Take my scarf." She handed me a light blue scarf that actually matched my tan blazer. "Your cough sounded bad this morning and you should be careful with this cold weather."

"Thank you, I'll bring this back next time." I slid it over my shoulders and gave her one more hug before leaving the old, musty smelling building. The metal handles on the door chilled my fingers as I pressed my way out into the blustery air. I'd forgotten my own scarf in the morning routine, but found myself grateful for evidence that what I was fighting for was worth it—a connected, Honeybrook community that cared. Pulling open the door to my car, I got in and drove to the nearest coffee shop. If I couldn't drink liquor, I'd at least be able to drink something warm.

Later that afternoon, I sat in the mayor's office in an ugly, coffee-stained, striped chair and tapped the top of my laptop, wishing I hadn't agreed to the annual meeting list. Because I had no building, the follow up meeting would be held at his office, and we'd be fighting on his turf now.

The mayor walked in, looking awkwardly happy.

"Leslie, good to have you here." He wiped the bald spot on the top of his head before sinking into his huge swivel chair and letting out a long sigh. "So, I've given this predicament a lot of thought."

I partially slid one foot in and out of my blue heels under the table, bracing myself for whatever else he would say.

"I feel like we've been chipping away at a problem too big for both of us, by building affordable housing. If I approve this, you'll want zoning for a senior living facility next. And why did you start clearing the ground on unapproved land?"

I forced myself to sit back calmly. "I'm only leveling it. And we have to face problems, not run away from them." I knew that sounded a little cliché, especially since I'd dodged my own problems by nearly drowning myself in liquor, but at least I faced my problems now—all of them.

"Leslie—" The mayor looked at me, sounding just like Jeremy when he said my name, and for a moment, we were both in the year 1992. I was eighteen and he was much younger. I wore a dusty pink dress for my family's summer party, and my hair had grown even longer that year.

I held a beer in my hand and rolled my eyes at Jeremy, Mayor Rosewater's son, as we stood in my family's backyard away from the adults who might catch us underage drinking. "No, I won't go out with you. Your uncle lost the game, and now we officially own a part of the beach."

"So, you won't go out with me?" Jeremy asked. "Because my uncle lost to your dad?"

"I only date winning stock. And my mother told me never to go out with the help." I knew that was a dumb and snooty reason. Jeremy had started working for my dad a few months ago for unknown reasons. I didn't find him attractive nor kind. I couldn't tell him that, though. I pulled my salon-dyed blond hair to the side and walked away to the table where a lovely spread of cheese and crackers and other hors d'oeuvres awaited me. An old friend and I chatted for almost an hour before Jeremy came back, this time drunk. I'd egged him on, more than I ever thought possible. And I had paid for it.

"I never want to see him again!" I sobbed to Dad later that night.

Dad nodded. "It's okay, sweetie. You won't have to see Jeremy again. He hasn't been doing his job right anyway."

I knew Dad sent people "away" before, and now I wanted him to do that for me. One month later to the day, Jeremy wasn't just away, he was dead. I didn't know that's how my dad handled business, but I initiated the request, and I blamed myself for it.

And for those reasons, I now grew sweaty in my seat, hoping the mayor wouldn't bring it up.

"Mayor, don't do it for me, do it for Honeybrook," I pleaded. "People are freezing."

"Don't give me that." Mayor Rosewater peered down his nose at me. "So are the people in Alaska right now. But they've figured it out and the rest of Honeybrook will figure it out too."

"Shouldn't we help them do just that?" I leaned forward.

The mayor stood, towering over me, his face turning red. "Leslie, you might outlive me, but I'll stay mayor of this town if the only thing I do in office is make sure you learn what it's like to lose what you love."

*Losing. Loss. Loser.* Unexpected heat burned in me even hotter. "Mayor, I've lost three children and my husband! How dare—" I choked up and covered my face with one hand. The tears flowed faster than I could wipe them away and the mayor looked away from me.

"And?" The mayor challenged.

"My building," I sputtered. "My health."

"But you don't know what it's like to bury your hope. Lose everything that matters."

"What do you think my two sons and daughter were?" I shouted. "What do you want to take from me, Mayor?"

"What did my son lose, Leslie?" The mayor stood up and stared down at me.

My heart grew cold and nearly stopped. I couldn't answer that question without bringing up the summer party and my harsh words that had egged him on. I was never even able to call a lawyer because of the part I'd played in the accident. I'd asked for Jeremy to be sent away, and I'd never forgiven myself for that.

"You've become so kind and involved in your adult years, with your Chancellor Homes foundations and the Hope for the Homeless commercial you have on TV." The mayor laced his fingers together. "Maybe it might touch your heart to know that my brother, Sam, is in the hospital. He's been busy, probably pushing himself too hard."

I felt my fingers and toes grow numb. "Yes." *Sam Rosewater is probably organizing one awful concert, agreeing to help hurt me and Candy... because...* my mouth went dry. After all, Sam had lost the bet, not the mayor. Like I thought, Sam had contacts, ones that could hurt Candy. Sweat dripped down my back.

"He's lost a lot too," the mayor said.

I could barely swallow.

"He might not live through the month."

I could practically smell the cheese dip from the summer party all those years before and taste the cheap, smuggled beer.

"I'll grant you zoning when you've lost everything that matters."

I finally swallowed hard. To my knowledge, I was the only person with any written evidence of Dad's notions about Jeremy, and for the sake of my safety and my family, I had to keep it that way.

"No deal." I heard the words coming from my mouth. "I've lost enough to fight for what I have, Mayor." I wiped under my eyes one last time. "So, we have to reach an agreement for Chancellor Homes, not Leslie Chancellor, formerly Leslie St. John."

"Would you risk losing that much?" the mayor asked. "Just to help the people of Honeybrook?"

I remembered how Candy's Rob-like curls had blown in the wind while she took New York by storm. "I promised my husband," I whispered.

# Act II: Cameras

# Chapter 9: Candy

"**P**ROMISE WE'LL GET A single from Grace Unchained?"
I asked Chris in the hallway at school.

"I think you guys have a really good shot," Chris said. "Randy told me a talent scout was in the audience, and they're having some meetings this week."

I started bouncing up and down in front of my locker. "They'll probably say yes, right? We sang with Grayson Lee!" Dreams of being a celebrity singer floated through my head, as I imagined the lights on me and my name being announced over the loudspeaker. Country music star Candy Chancellor. I loved it.

Chris laughed and pulled me into a hug. "I hope they say yes to this sweet little firecracker. But let's wait and see. And pray."

I nodded and adjusted my backpack as we both walked further down the hallway. *The Fruit of Spirit included joy,* I thought. Maybe I could show fruit? A little nudge kicked at me as I remembered Mom's attempted prayer, but I pushed it away. What did Mom know about music anyway?

Mom stayed quiet all that evening and mechanically microwaved dinner for the two of us. We ate in silence. I desperately wanted to escape the deafening quiet and play the guitar upstairs, even though I knew I should study for the SATs to score in the green on the practice test in a few days.

"I'm going to go study for the SATs," I announced after I shoved the last piece of honey glazed turkey in my mouth. "Thanks for dinner."

"Uh, Candy." Mom pushed her veggies around with her fork. "I know I told you that you could stay with the band if you scored green on the next SATs, but for now, I think just staying in the band without being in the spotlight might be the best option."

"Mom, how could you? We could be asked to make a single!" I shouted and pushed back from the table, making it wobble. "With Grace Unchained!" I stormed away from her. "You're totally not being fair at all!"

Mom rubbed the bridge of her nose. "I know about the single, honey, but there are some things going on at work that would make producing a single dangerous for you and the band."

I froze in place. "What do you mean?"

Mom twisted a piece of hair with her finger. "Making a single that could become very popular, or performing in Virginia, might put you at risk for something I don't want to happen to you, okay? I'll talk to Chris and see what he says, but for now, I think we should table it."

Mom's boardroom talk made my skin crawl, and I felt tears burning my eyes. Why did her life always ruin mine? "This is my dream, Mom." I sniffled. "How dangerous could it be?"

Mom blinked at me. "It could cost a lot of people's dreams, honey."

# Chapter 2: Candy

T HE NEXT MORNING, MOM'S coughing kept her in bed long enough to worry me. She usually struggled through her mornings, sometimes even needing a break before making us breakfast. But now, as I eavesdropped on the painful sounding cough from the other side of the door, I wondered what really went on. Was it really the business or was it her health?

"It's all coming back, Chris." I heard Mom choke out the words on the phone. "It's been almost thirty years, and I can't run from it anymore."

I pressed my ear closer to the door. What in the world could my sweetheart of a mom be worried about from thirty years ago?

"If they offer her a single, I can't let her produce it. That would make matters worse."

Chris had to be talking, but Mom kept clearing her throat.

"Okay, I'll see what she says."

I heard the creaking of the mattress as Mom got out of bed, and I quickly tiptoed back to my room.

"You can come in," Mom called.

I froze mid-skid down the hallway and shuffled back. "Good morning," I said.

Mom raised an eyebrow at me. "Good morning. So, tell me, what did you learn from the other side of the door?"

I noticed the pile of used tissues on her nightstand and the half empty glass of water. Mom switched off her oxygen tank and began to set up her daytime portable one. She moved her hair back as she adjusted the tubes and began to carry it around the room as she got dressed.

"You were talking about the single," I said.

"Yes." Mom took a black jumpsuit out of her closet and tossed it on her bed.

"And you kind of still don't want me to do it," I added.

Mom gave me a glance as she took a hair tie from her nightstand and twisted her hair into a low ponytail. "But you really want to make the single."

"I thought that's what Jesus wanted me to do."

Mom took off her pink robe and reached for her jumpsuit. "So, does Jesus want you to obey your parents or witness?"

"That's not a fair question!" I didn't mean to shout. "God says both."

"Okay," Mom said slowly. "So, I'm going to give the decision back to you. With only knowing I said it *might* be dangerous, would you make the single if you were offered one?"

The chance to make the single surged through me again, and all my dreams felt like they were glowing city lights dancing around me. I could envision myself performing on the famous Grand Ole Opry stage in Nashville, having my debut album, and touching souls one song at a time. I wanted this. I wished I hadn't overheard Mom's prayer and, in the moment, self-control escaped me. Frustrated heat filled me as Mom switched from her pajamas to her work clothes.

"I'd want to make the single," I blurted. She wasn't ruining this with her nerves this time.

Despite Mom's years in the boardroom and her executive experience, the hurt showed in her face. I tried to ignore it, though. Didn't she know that spreading the Gospel was important?

# Chapter 3: Leslie

I COULD HOPE THAT Grace Unchained said no. I reached for a coffee mug in the kitchen cabinet. If Candy wanted to make the single, I'd have to protect her the best way I knew how. The Rosewaters would love to retaliate with Candy having an "accident" on stage. I could smell it. Even if the Rosewaters knew where we lived, revenge wouldn't be good enough unless others witnessed it, or as in the case with my parents, read about it with pictures. At home, at least she'd be with me–the doors were locked, and I could track her every move on her cell phone. I thought about making sure that if they made the single, it never saw the light of day by somehow having the file "accidentally" destroyed. I stood in front of the coffee maker, waiting for the warm drink to fill my mug, and chided myself for the childish thought. After all, the demolition method was how my parents had handled things when I was a teen, and I never believed it was a good choice.

I took a sip of coffee and went to the couch to set up my laptop. Ordinarily, I would have worked in my office, but feeling tired already, I stayed on the couch and clicked the links to the video chats to hear updates about the business– the business who knew nothing about my past. And for those reasons, I had to stay in the present.

"We don't have the money," Wendy said in a garbled voice as the computer glitched.

"We don't have the money for what?" I asked.

"This New York project could send us in the yellow, Leslie," Mike said. "We can continue to acquire land, but with the economy, we might not get the return we're looking for."

"Where are we now?" I asked.

"We're still in the green," Mike said.

I started laughing. "Well, then, we keep buying and selling land, guys. That's what we do."

Mike's face held annoyance, even over the computer, and he turned off his screen. Seriously, that man had problems with a woman being his boss. I sighed and opened my email to check for the list of potential parcels of land I could acquire in the next few months.

"Thanks, Wendy, I have it," I said. "I'll review these and get back to you all tomorrow."

# Chapter 4: Candy

I BLINKED AT MOM as she sat down on the couch next to Chris, this time, reclining back to sleep for real. She hadn't really rested post-fire, and she kept pushing off what seemed to be an impending cold. I sat across from them.

"Chris." Mom leaned against his shoulder, almost too close for my liking. "The mayor is talking about Jeremy again."

Chris stopped stroking Mom's arm. "Why?"

"Rob's gone, and he's always wanted to get even with me. I cleared the land to move ahead with the project." Mom moved away and sat up. "And Rosewater is moving ahead with what he's wanted to do a long time ago. He could never hold this many mandatory meetings with Rob alive, and Rob would never have allowed Chancellor Homes to be tainted with my past."

For the first time in my life, I witnessed the color drain from Chris' face. "I don't know why he's taking it out on you," Chris said. "I mean, it wasn't your fault."

"But I started it, and it would never have happened if–" Mom stopped talking and looked at me. "Candy, could you order dinner for us, please?"

"Who's Jeremy?" I leaned forward in my chair.

I caught the look between Chris and Mom. "Mayor Rosewater's son," Mom said.

I squinted my eyes a little. "What does he have to do with Chancellor Homes?"

"Nothing," Mom said. "Chris and I are just reminiscing. Please order dinner now." Mom's voice came out soft and tired.

I didn't believe her, not even a little bit. As I ordered pizza, I wondered what Chris and Mom weren't saying.

Thirty minutes later, I sat on the steps, waiting for the arrival of burritos, pizza, and a salad. I saw the driver from down the road and stood at the door so I could give him the cash Mom gave me as a bonus tip. He wasn't in our driveway yet when I heard Mom groaning in the other room.

I walked down the hallway and peeped into the living room.

"Les', they're supposed to help," Chris said. "If Jeremy is back in the picture, you need to take your evening anxiety meds too."

Mom's face twisted in pain. "I took it, but I don't think the second dose is going to stay down." The barely audible whisper frightened me. "Oh my gosh, Chris!" Mom gripped Chris by the arms and pressed her forehead onto his chest, leaving nail marks on his skin.

"Candy, grab the trash can," Chris said over his shoulder, trying to steady Mom.

The doorbell rang. Dinner. I froze, glancing from Mom to the front door, not sure where to go first. Would he just leave it? Or did I have to be there? Mom reached across the living room table and grabbed the popcorn bowl. She tossed the remaining kernels on the table and held the bowl to her face as she became violently ill. I froze in my spot. I hadn't seen her both sober and this sick since

Daddy was alive. Chris seemed to be shaken up too. He wouldn't let go of her, even after the event unfolded.

"It's way too strong," Mom choked. "I can't take it."

The doorbell rang again, but Mom's breathing had changed. "I just need air."

Chris fumbled for the tubes Mom had taken out when she'd been sick. They'd been carelessly tossed somewhere over the side of the couch.

"Better?" Chris asked.Mom groaned. "Can't I request to take something else?"

Chris glanced at me. "Can you please get the door?"

My legs felt wobbly as I walked to the door. I opened it to find Nate carrying our entire dinner.

"Nate?" I asked, taking the dinner from his hands.

"Hey, Candy," Nate said. "How's it going?"

I didn't even know how to answer that, so I said, "We're hanging in there."

"Cool," Nate said. "It's good to see you."

"Thanks." I heard a shout from Mom and caught a glance from Nate. "My mom is just a little under the weather," I explained, then handed him the tip. "See you at practice?" I asked.

"Sure thing." Nate jogged down the steps, and I shut the door.

"Candy, can you please grab some ice water and ginger ale from the fridge?" Chris asked. "I don't know if she'll be able to do dinner or not."

I complied, but as I did, I noticed that Mom did in fact look smaller, almost too small. *That phone conversation Mom had with Chris the other morning... had I missed something besides the anxiety? Had I been a little too wrapped up?*

"Honey," Chris said and helped Mom sit up. "You're going to have to sip this slowly, okay?"

Mom nodded. "Thanks."

As I sat back down in the living room chair, I thought about how much Chris helped Mom and how much she relied on us for her healing after addiction. If we both left her to make a single, what would happen? Would she relapse? Would she be so sick the hospital would call us? Would she make it to the hospital? Or would something worse happen and the police would call us saying they found her? Would I lose my mom?

"That was so gross," Mom said, leaning back a little on the couch. "I'm so sorry."

"It wasn't your fault," Chris assured Mom. "We have to find the right medication for you."

Mom closed her eyes and leaned against his shoulder. "You're right." Those were Mom's last words before she shivered and fell asleep on Chris.

I wanted to cry. I couldn't leave my only family on earth to make a single. Not when she needed me and Chris to help her heal from the fire and manage her new health issues. Plus, after New York, the doctor had cautioned her against traveling for a while. And now this Jeremy business, whatever that was.

"Candy, can you put my dinner in the fridge?" Chris asked. "I don't want to wake your mom."

I nodded.

Mom kept shivering and Chris reached for a throw blanket. But under the added weight, Mom immediately started panicking.

"Stop," Mom moaned.

Chris started to take the blanket off, and I moved closer to the couch to comfort her.

Mom gripped the blanket tighter. "It was a mistake." Mom's hands shook at her sides, and Chris moved quickly to reposition her.

Chris' eyes grew damp. "Did she ever tell you about that?"

"No." I felt myself getting frustrated. "What mistake?"

"It wasn't a complete mistake, but it's the exact reason why she can't be home alone."

And in that moment, watching my mom take her next breath on an oxygen machine and calling out into the dimly lit living room, I decided I couldn't leave her to make a single. *She* was my single family member, and I loved her. More than music. My heart broke as I thought about it, but in my heart of hearts, I knew she was too sick to be left alone—nerves or not. The fire had scarred her and so did whatever mysterious not-complete-mistake.

But if I was going to give up the single, I needed to know about the mistake.

"Chris?" I asked softly.

Chris stood and took the rancid-smelling popcorn bowl to the trash can. I followed, dying to know more.

"What happened with Mom and Jeremy?" I asked.

Chris didn't say anything for a moment, but began to rinse out the rest of the dirty bowl in the sink, using the spray attachment from the faucet as he did. "If your mom didn't tell you, it's not for me to say."

Mom just moaned from the other room. I didn't realize she could overhear us. "Please. Talking about it makes it worse." She leaned back on the pillows slowly. "I have to meet with him soon, and Jeremy will be a part of the conversation, I'm sure." A few tears ran down Mom's eyes. "And if he is..." Mom trailed off and resumed crying.

Chris' face melted into one of deep concern as Mom sobbed into one of the couch pillows. All questions I had about making the single were answered too. I didn't need to know the story to show love. I just had to see Mom's desperate need for it and do it. Which, in this case, meant being here for her, since that was the only way I saw Mom healing– and the Mom I prayed for.

# Chapter 5: Candy

T HAT NIGHT, I STOOD in front of the mirror and imagined saying no to Grace Unchained. Mom and the mayor clearly had history, even if I didn't know all the details. I sat on my bed and pulled my guitar closer to my chest.

I knew that spreading the Gospel meant living it as well. I should obey and live out my faith, even if that meant I shared Jesus with Mom first and stayed on YouTube.

After a hot shower and a good cry, I felt better. We'd get through this. God had always pulled us through the tough stuff. I dried my hair with a towel and yanked on a pair of joggers and a t-shirt. I practiced saying no in the steamy mirror again. I'd have to stay on YouTube and tell them that family came first. That was obedience. Tears came as I thought about it, and it seemed like my dreams swirled down the drain with the soapy suds from my shower. But it had to be this way. I loved Mom too much to let something dangerous happen to her or to me or to us. And to some extent, without saying anything more, she had other points. What if my grades only got worse? I stuck my deodorant back on the cabinet shelf and reconsidered everything again.

Inside the enormous studio Mom built for us, I sat at the baby grand piano and thought about the New York trip–the hotel, the concert, Grayson Lee. Sure, life had been hard and kept changing, but I kept changing too. Was I about to watch our band dissolve and die? The last of my dreams threatened to whither. This time last year, I wouldn't have cared about the Chozen Band or bearing fruit, but now I decided I at least wanted to obey the Bible. I needed to show love to Mom. I didn't want to witness to a million people while leaving my only family hurting and alone. One last song danced across my heart and I jotted it down.

If I were a flower/
I'd tilt my head towards Heaven.
If I were a flower/
Made to bloom /
My life would worship You/
If I were a flower/
You'd show me Your power/
I'd last through all my storms.
So here I am/
A fragile flower/
Needing Your power/
In this hour.
God, help me bloom/
Tilt my head/
Heal my heart/
Plant this flower/
Close to You

"God, please help us," I whispered as I wrote the final words on the page. "Please." My heart wavered like the flowers in the wind, and my lyrics exposed every part of me. I re-read them. I meant them. Every last word. But would they come true? I closed the lid to the piano, left my notebook on top, and walked out of the studio. I couldn't let myself think about it anymore.

# Chapter 6: Leslie

I COULDN'T STOP SNEEZING and the words from the doctor came back to me. "COPD makes you more likely to pick up colds and infections. If you don't rest, you'll pick up way more than your share."

I sank into the couch with my laptop and scanned my emails. I hoped I wasn't coming down with anything. Did I catch it from that guy in the hotel? I honestly didn't have time to be sick. My scratchy throat didn't help matters. I clicked open the email from Wendy saying that the mayor wanted to meet again. I'd lost the paper he'd given me in the fire, so she had to be right. My heart sped up, and I subconsciously rubbed my ribs. I had at least two weeks this time to prepare my appeal for him. This many meetings back-to-back meant the one thing I feared–he was getting ready to either tell me no or he was going to get even with me once and for all.

I deleted junk emails and let my mind wander to Jack, the custodian, and how I wanted him to live in Honeybrook–along with so many other employees who'd been priced out of the area. Wendy lived in Ridge Creek and so did Susan. The only employee we had that I knew lived in Honeybrook was Mike. Rob wanted Honeybrook to be a place anyone and everyone could live. But as I sat against the pillows, looking out the window at our beach, it all seemed like an unattainable dream. The setting sun warmed my heart a little, but it only reminded me of reality. I was running out of time. I knew how dirty the mayor could be.

It hurt to swallow, so I stood to find a lozenge for my throat. A barking cough escaped me, and I leaned against the counter, wishing my days weren't so painful and my nights weren't so long. I wished as hard as I could, but still that night, I tossed and turned as I slowly started to burn with fever. Sweat dripped down my back, and I only hoped the cold would be a short one. After all, I had to organize a slideshow in the morning to beg the mayor to approve my appeal in two weeks. Homelessness had gone up, but more people were working. *People*.

A fever dream evoked the terrifying scene from the summer party. I saw Jeremy Rosewater's red, sweaty face and my pink dress drenched in blood. But that was the least of my worries. I heard people screaming, including myself. Muggy heat surrounded us, and everyone shouted in fear of Jeremy's outburst. Then, Mayor Rosewater held Candy over an open flame and she kicked around, struggling to break free. "You lost, Leslie!" the old man shouted maniacally in my dream. "You've finally lost everything!" The words echoed, and he laughed as he came chasing after me, eyes wild while he lunged to hold me over a flame too.

I sat up, panting. The Rosewaters wouldn't take Candy from me. There had to be some way around it, a safer way.

# Chapter 7: Candy

CHRIS ASKED TO HOLD a meeting with us in the studio that Friday, and despite my new personal resolution, I agreed. Nate hadn't been able to make it. Mom let everyone in precisely at four, but her awful coughing made Scott and Nina keep their eyes lowered as I escorted them up to the studio. Everyone remained silent for a full beat.

We heard Mom sneeze from downstairs, and Chris shot me a compassionate expression.

"Okay, guys, I know we've been holding our breath for the past few days. I don't doubt for a minute that God has a plan for us in the middle of this, and I have good news for you. Grace Unchained Records had someone in the crowd like we hoped and expected. They'd like to offer you guys a single."

I clenched my hands together in my lap, and my heart skipped a beat. Weren't those my dreams? Yes. But they'd shattered now, after I finally saw how scared and sick my mom really was. That broken piece of my heart stayed patched up like plaster on one of our Chancellor Homes. Only that particular piece of plaster work never dried well at all. It always threatened to crack again.

"Candy?" Chris snapped me back to the deal.

"Yes?"

"The single?"

I looked up, first at Nina, then at Scott. They were both so happy, and I was going to let them down. I closed my eyes and took a breath. "I can't do it," I admitted.

I felt everyone's eyes on me, and my heart fell to my feet.

"Are you sure about this?" Chris asked me, eyebrows raised in concern.

"I'm sure." I bit my lip, feeling wobbly as I did.

The warmth in the room vanished into a cold, distant one I never expected. Not from Chris, but from Nina and Scott. They'd trusted me to push the band to the limelight, to be a part of the team, and I'd just let them down.

"Honey, are you sure you don't want to take a day or two to think about it?" Chris moved closer to my stool.

Scott and Nina looked at me.

"Please?" Scott begged.

"I don't need any time to think about it." As I said the words, tiny pieces of my heart fell. "Mom doesn't just have a cold. The fire made her lungs worse, and she needs me. I'm sorry, I can't." I stared at my feet as I remembered Mom's painful breathing emergencies, nightmares, and panic attacks.

"I'll have to let Grace Unchained know," Chris said the words slowly as he stood. "You guys are dismissed." Chris said them with a finality, as if we'd never have this opportunity again. And somewhere, I knew he was probably right.

# Chapter 8: Candy

I T WAS USELESS TO keep writing songs that were going nowhere, so I stuffed Daddy's blue travel journal into my drawer and focused on what mattered most—my family. Sure, Chris was here when we needed him, but only I could comfort Mom when her nightmares became too real for her.

*Maybe being a famous singer was too much of a longshot,* I thought as I brushed my teeth and got ready for bed. *Maybe I had hoped too hard.* I spit in the sink, wiped my mouth with the back of my hand, and began combing my curls softly, trying not to let myself think about any more tunes. I didn't stream any music as I got ready for bed, and before I hopped under the covers, I slipped my guitars in their cases and put them in my closet—out of sight, and out of mind. I had more things to think about now, like actually doing well in school and making sure that my mom and I would stay afloat.

To be honest, I didn't even know if the band would want to perform for YouTube with me, especially since I let them down. They'd left without even looking at me. Without a band, there was no music career. I'd buried the absolute last of my dreams. My tears soaked my pillow as I took in the reality of my decisions. I'd given up the chance of a lifetime because I wanted to live like Jesus. I wanted my mom not to be scared or sick. I wanted to show love. I only hoped I'd done it right this time.

◆◇◆ ◆◆◆ ◆◇◆

At school the next day, Chris took me aside first thing and told me he understood, especially with how unsteady Mom's recovery had been. He also told the band that since Mom was sick, the studio had to be off limits for a while. Of course, that meant that we weren't practicing, not even for YouTube. My life felt like Honeybrook High, homework, and bed, but on repeat. I trudged to my classes, somewhat grateful Chris had extended grace that morning.

"Grace Unchained will never give us another chance," Nina moaned as she slammed her locker door shut, and we got ready to change classes after lunch.

I hung my head and looked at Scott, who stood next to me. "You can get another singer?" I suggested.

"They loved your voice," Scott said. "You're the voice behind the Chozen Band."

I tried to hide my face a little behind my locker door as I felt tears coming into my eyes. If God had chosen me, why wasn't He making this easier? Why did it feel like a fight to bear fruit?

Chris, who had been monitoring the halls after lunch, found us huddled together and joined our small group. He knew we still had music on our minds. "Guys, I know that the past few days have been really hard, but can you all come with me for a moment to the auditorium?"

We followed, but I stayed keenly aware of the fact that I was missing moments with my SAT tutor, who had more of my attention since I was not going to be a famous singer. I took a seat in the red plush chair and waited for Chris to speak.

"It's no one's fault about the single," Chris began. "We know that God works all things for the good of those who love Him, who are called according to His purpose." Chris quoted Scripture. What was my purpose now? To be a better caregiver? To take over Chancellor Homes?

"Grace Unchained rescinded their offer," Chris said, and the words fell on my heart like heavy boulders–painful and unmoving.

Nina glared at me, but Scott didn't say a word. I squirmed in my chair and tried to avoid their guilt-inducing gazes. It was my fault. I'd chosen family over fame, and now I'd probably never get the opportunity to be onstage again. My eyes watered as I looked at the wooden stage where I'd rehearsed in front of Chris when I first came to Honeybrook High. So much had happened since then. The unbearable silence in the room raised the unspoken question. "What would happen now?"

After school, I sat on my bed, scrolled through social media and posted an old selfie of me with my guitar using the hashtags **#honeybrookhigh** and **#music**. Casual posting was more my thing, but after our performance with *We the Guilty*, I tended to get lots of likes anyway. Maybe because I was the only one from the band who consistently posted on social media. I scrolled through a few other posts, but stopped when I came to a picture of Anna. She had one hand over her stomach, but didn't smile in her picture.

**Heading to Honey-Tech in the fall. Here's to mom-school life.**

My heart ached for her as I stared out at the frost-covered lawn, courtesy of February. I didn't know when she was due, but I was grateful she'd chosen to keep the baby.

I also didn't know if Ms. Michelle had agreed to let Mom foot the hospital bill. Despite me not liking Anna so much before, I truly felt sorry for her now, but I also understood her a little bit. She had talent as a drummer, and she tossed everything away in one single night. Maybe that's why my heart still broke a little from giving up my big chance in one single night. I felt called to sing, but at the same time, I knew it hurt Mom. Did I hear God wrong?

The next day in the kitchen, I did Bible study and ordered breakfast on our beloved delivery app. I let out a long sigh. My lyrics could die in a shoebox or they could be sung to the world. I didn't know. I spent the day with Mom, catching up on movies, trying not to think about tomorrow.

"Can you refill the humidifier, please?" Mom asked me, voice crackly from her lung injuries and intermittent sleeping.

I took the water component from the humidifier and refilled it, hoping that somewhere, Mom would make a miraculous full recovery. I reconnected the device and allowed the smart settings to do the rest of the work. I took a glance at Mom. After three days, she still hadn't shaken her cold. In fact, she seemed worse.

# Chapter 9: Leslie

E VERY SOOTHING DRINK, LOZENGE, nasal spray, or syrup wasn't helping this cold. Even though I'd been told that I'd catch more colds and I might not get over a cold the way I used to, it worried me. What would cure my colds now? I sat on the edge of the couch with a few tissues in hand and wiped my nose, hoping that I could breathe better now. The fever hadn't broken either, which only made matters worse. A notification on my phone alerted me that the carseat for the baby I picked out would be delivered in two weeks. I closed my eyes, grateful one thing had gone right today. The doorbell rang and I wearily forced myself up from the couch to answer it.

Chris.

*We still hadn't talked about the baby. And would he think it was a bad idea now that I'm permanently sick?*

"Leslie?" Chris seemed shocked and his eyes lingered on my messy hair. "Candy told me you had a cold, but are you sure you're okay?"

I nodded. "I just need sleep," I said, leaning against the doorframe. "What brings you over?" I motioned him in.

"I wanted to check on you after school, that's all." Chris followed me down the hallway and back to the living room where we both took seats. I clicked on the television.

"Thank you," I sighed. "I'm still alive." My tone came out as dry as I wanted it to.

"Where's Candy?" Chris asked.

"I honestly don't know what she's up to at the moment." I started getting up from the couch to look for her, but began a series of deep coughs and couldn't stop.

"Inhaler?" Chris asked.

I couldn't answer him.

"Urgent care?" Chris moved closer to me as I fumbled with even more tissues.

"Mom?" Candy called from upstairs. "Are you okay?"

*So that's where she was.*

Chris reached over and placed a hand on my forehead. "You're burning up. We're going to the emergency room."

I could only squeak the word okay.

The seven minute drive to the emergency room with Chris and Candy was filled with my labored breathing and intermittent coughing. I had so much phlegm in my throat, I could hardly get it out.

"Les'" Chris' eyebrows furrowed in concern as he drove. "Here's a tissue."

As I tried to clear my airway, I realized I'd left my oxygen at home in the rush to leave. That explained my strained breathing.

"Candy, can you tell the people inside we need help?" Chris asked as soon as we parked in front of the sign that said "Emergency."

Tears were running down Candy's face, but she nodded. People came quickly, at least I heard them before everything went black.

# Chapter 10: Candy

A NURSE WHEELED MOM into a small emergency room on a stretcher, and I followed, my knees wobbly. I couldn't tell if Mom had come to or not, but she was ashen and silent as I peeked over the shoulder of the nurse wheeling her back. I tried to force my legs to follow her behind the scary curtain.

"Honey, give us a minute," the nurse said, stopping me. "You can check back in very soon, okay? We'll come and get you."

I sighed and called Scott while I walked out to the waiting room with Chris. As soon as Scott said hello, I blurted out all my panicked feelings.

"Woah, Candy!" Scott said after I finished my rant. "It's all going to be fine. We know your mom is sick, so maybe she needs more help or something."

"Scott, I'm scared," I said, leaning against a cold, tiled wall. "I'm scared I'm going to lose my mom in the same hospital I lost my dad. Her lips turned blue!" That was more vulnerable than I had planned. "Can you please come over?"

"I'm in the middle of practicing for the SATs at the moment," Scott said. "Can I pop over later?"

"Scott!" I shouted and people looked at me in the waiting room. "What if I don't get to take her home? I'm scared now!"

"Do you have an update on her?"

"Scott, you'd know if you were here."

"Candy, remember the winter carnival when your mom came? My mom told me I could only go if I promised to come back and study for the SATs. I had to honor that the way you're honoring your mom and staying with her. Obedience was one of the promises I made to both my mom and my dad, not that you've paid much attention to the fact he's gone."

"Why are you making this about you?" I hissed into the speaker. "Mom is in the hospital–again!"

"Just let me study, Candy." Scott sounded tired and I wanted to choke him through the phone.

"Well, I won't interrupt your studies," I said coldly, then hung up. I couldn't believe him. He couldn't come over at a time like this?

"Candy." Chris lowered my phone with one finger, seemingly unaware of my argument with Scott. "Mom has been through so much." Chris looked away from me and bit his knuckle. "She's been sick since she started talking to the mayor again. I think this is more than a cold."

I said nothing for a full beat and watched as he shifted in his chair.

"This could be mixed with a panic attack," Chris sighed.

A nurse came out and motioned for us to follow her back to see Mom.

I let my tears of complete terror fall as I followed her to see Mom, who lay asleep with the lightest blanket covering her. My heart seemingly beat to the soundtrack of a horror movie inside me. How many hospital visits would there be? The sound of the machines always gave me the jitters, and I hated the sterile smell. If Daddy were alive, he'd take us on a vacation for a month so Mom could rest. Without Daddy, Mom hadn't given herself those kinds of luxuries. Daddy would have said the strain of work had been too much. But Mom was Chancellor Homes, and now I stood there, watching as she received IV fluids and medication. She seemed groggy, but at least she was awake.

A nurse walked in, got some information from me, and I tapped my foot against the tile floor. She told us Mom's fever still hadn't broken. Mom sat up and began squeezing her stomach, but didn't say anything.

"Honey, they're going to help your stomach," Chris said in a soft voice.

Mom just kept gripping her middle.

"Okay," Chris acknowledged Mom's unspoken pain and sat down next to her. He squeezed her hand, which was something he'd do on and off for the rest of the night since the doctors wanted to keep her for observation. Mom's cold had pushed her into a COPD exacerbation, and she needed more help breathing, but she'd also had a panic attack too. One that had been brought on by her health and work.

The night at the hospital was filled with deep moans from Mom. When she wasn't receiving medication, someone always popped in to either calm her down, offer her a snack or water, or distract her. Chris tried to calm Mom down when the anxiety started to eat at her by playing music on his phone. When that didn't work, nurses came in and soothed her by changing the television, adding more blankets, or brushing her hair–a technique they said stimulated her scalp and calmed her more than we expected.

By morning, Mom's fever broke and despite her make-up-streaked face, she looked almost like her usual self. She took to the breakfast fruit cups for some reason and asked for more. Chris promised her more when we got home that day.

"The doctor said you've lost weight," Chris told Mom as soon as we got back inside. "You require more oxygen now, and you're going to have to rest."

Mom sighed, "I know."

Chris' expression softened. "I know your stomach is often your worst enemy, but the hospital did give you a few more fruit cups since you begged so nicely." They both laughed.

"I didn't think they'd let me take those home." Mom turned pink. "They were so good."

"You were the sweetest patient on the floor," Chris said and handed me the fruit cups.

"Thank you," Mom said and sat down on the sofa, motioning for me to sit down next to her. Her hair fell to one side, and she pulled me into a soft hug. "I'm sorry I scared you."

I nodded my response and placed the fruit cups on the table.

"And I'm sorry I pulled you into yet another ER trip," Mom told Chris.

Chris laughed. "After all these years, I'd be upset if you left me out."

"Wait, what other time did Mom go to the hospital with..." I tried to read both of their faces.

Mom flushed deep red now. "After your grandparents passed, your dad and Chris did their best to help me cope, but none of us knew I'd developed anxiety. Really, I'd had it before then, but it was magnified. So, to help me out, your dad would slip me drinks and cigarettes after classes."

"We thought your mom was better until she had a bad attack and needed meds." Chris sat down on the other side of Mom.

"One random day, before you were born, your dad and I welcomed a new family into one of our homes, and I came later that week to help them decorate it. They'd wanted a nautical-themed home, and I couldn't stop thinking about your grandparents' boating accident. I had such a severe attack, I couldn't move." Mom reached for the television remote. "The family freaked out, and your dad drove me to the hospital." Mom shook her head. "After I got my breath back, your dad and I decided I should take some meds for my nerves."

"Until..." Chris edged Mom on.

"Well, the meds didn't always work," Mom agreed. "And sometimes still don't. Before you were born, your dad, Chris and I took the ferry to New Jersey to explore some new land."

"And we learned that any boat is not a good idea for your mom." Chris softly rubbed Mom's shoulder.

"I had to be escorted off." Mom covered her face with her hand. "That was the first of a few times Chris came with us to the emergency room. I actually fainted for that one. And every time after that, Chris has always been at the hospital when I've had an emergency."

"They were all valid." Chris gave Mom a hug. "You've never gone to urgent care unless you truly couldn't breathe or couldn't stop getting sick to your stomach."

Mom shrugged. "Or I was in labor. But seriously, what would they do that I wouldn't do at home?"

Chris rolled his eyes. "They have medication, Leslie. Different medication to help you calm down."

Mom sighed. I knew this journey was hard on her, especially the medication part. But she needed us as she healed. That was crystal clear.

Later that day, Scott rang the doorbell. Notes of frustration pressed against my heart, and I didn't want to see him. He was too late. He hadn't stopped by "later" at all.

I yanked the door open, taking in his laidback posture. He tossed me his dimpled smile and shoved his phone in his pocket, but I didn't smile back. "Scott, I want us to take a break." The unplanned heated words flew out of my mouth.

He hadn't kept his word and stopped by last night or this morning. The day was practically over, and he hadn't even texted to check on how we were doing.

"What do you mean?" Scott's eyes widened.

"I mean, we should stop seeing each other for a while."

"What makes you say that?" Scott's eyes widened and he removed his cowboy hat, tossed his hair to the side, and shifted his stance a little.

"If the SATs and following all the rules are that important to you, then maybe that's what you should be doing. I never know if I'll wake up and have to take my mom to the hospital, but you seem to need to know exactly when you're doing everything. I don't understand why you couldn't drop everything and come over."

"Candy, I know you and your mom have been through a lot, and I care a lot about you both. And, I guess Ms. Leslie is well enough to give my mom a character reference for a new job, now that Dad's not here. I appreciate you coming to the funeral, though." Scott crossed his arms in defense. "But lately it's like you've totally forgotten what it's like to lose a parent or grieve or anything."

"What do you mean? I grieve Daddy every single day!" I raised my voice and clung onto the oak door for support.

"I mean, you make everything about you. You wanted to be famous and now that your mom is sick, you drop the entire band. What happened to music as an escape for you, Candy? Did you ever stop and think I might need that?" His words stopped me in my tracks. I couldn't win for losing.

"Scott."

"Yes?"

"Next time, I'll call you."

There was a brief silence as the windy air blew between us.

"Candy, I'll be expecting that call."

He jogged down the steps and walked down the driveway. Who needed boys now? Maybe Chris should exempt both of us from the Fruit of the Spirit Challenge. I definitely should be, now more than ever. I mean, clearly Mom and I needed support, and sure, maybe Scott did too. But his mom was healthy and mine fought for air to breathe.

# Chapter 11: Leslie

SITTING ACROSS FROM CHRIS the next evening in the living room should have calmed me, but it didn't. Restlessness coursed through every fiber of my being, making it so I couldn't stretch out on the couch. I felt less congested after the hospital stay, but my mind wouldn't let me relax. "Chris, Candy wants to go for the big time, and you and I both know that means she'd have to be away from me for that. If it's not a single, it will be another concert or a mini tour. She wants the stage."

"Leslie, you're going to have to trust God that He will take care of Candy and you," he started slowly, eyeing me closely. I knew I had pushed back on faith so hard in college that Chris really stopped sharing. Rob had accepted later, but I still hadn't wanted to take part in it. Even now that Candy had asked Jesus into her heart, I'd been open to the idea of God, but still refused to commit my whole life to Him. Why was Chris pushing faith now? My heart took two heavy thuds against my chest. I stood and walked to the recliner where he seemed far too casual for our conversation.

"Chris, don't go there with me." I didn't mean to shout. "Tell me, where was God when my parents died, huh? Why didn't he walk on water to save them? Where was God when my husband took his last breath in a mangled

SUV? Where was God when my baby didn't cry? Where was God when the other two wouldn't cry either, and I was the one in tears? You've lived a status quo life, Chris. I've–" I placed one hand over my chest and leaned over him. "Every time I needed God–" I burst into tears, and Chris immediately stood to hug me. There wasn't anything we could say in that moment. The pain in the room could be touched. I trembled in Chris' arms as the brief thought about only being two months clean flitted through my head.

"God was there," Chris whispered. "He just didn't give you the answer that you wanted."

"And why would I commit my life to a God who took everyone I loved?" The shouting became higher, almost in his ear as tears rolled down my face. "I can trust that if I keep Candy with me, she'll be safe. If I let her out of my sight, she could get hurt."

"God loves you, Leslie." Chris kept holding me. "Life with Jesus is the safest commitment in the world."

"I don't want God to take my last baby!" I shouted. "Please, God, no!""Les'." Chris gave me a confused glance. "God isn't taking Candy. She has talent, but she told me–"

I cut him off. "Just stop it, Chris." I closed my eyes. "You don't get it."

Chris looked like he wanted to tell me more, but I didn't want to hear it. My brain had to work with what I already had.

I'd said one other desperate prayer just like that one, but whatever faith I had was about to die because letting Candy go meant surrendering all to God. All I could hope for was a breath of mercy that God wouldn't take her away, that maybe I'd live long enough to see her get married and have children, that maybe He'd forgive me for the Rosewater situation. But, I knew I didn't deserve it and my heart shattered because it wasn't the trendy band that was "guilty--it was me.

"Chris, if I don't let Candy make that single, she'll hate me for not giving her the chance. I'll be 'that' mom who is 'ruining' her life. But you don't know Rosewater. If I let her go, I could really lose her."

Chris's eyebrows wrinkled in hesitation for a brief second, and he softly ran his hand over my hair. "Whether or not Candy makes the single, can't you give faith one more shot?"

I squinted my eyes at him, and I knew his question ran deeper than that. Half a question came to mind, but it never fully surfaced. I stared into Chris' deep, trusting eyes. This was the last time he would ask me to trust God, and I knew that. Would my heart beat alive with faith or was it already dead? And if so, could God resurrect the heart of a broken woman like me?

# Chapter 12: Leslie

I NEEDED A MOM-DAUGHTER day with me and Candy. She hadn't been herself over the past few weeks, fire or no fire. I ran my fingers through my shortened hair and took a seat at my desk at home. The world outside looked cold, and despite being home, the winter chill still seemed to hang in the air. I reached down and turned on the space heater. I also desperately needed to meet with marketing, but Candy and I needed to talk. I thought about how she made me proud, yet how I worried about her because I loved her that much. I also needed an assistant to help me keep things running. I reached for the phone and dialed Heather from human resources.

"Hello?"

"This is Leslie Chancellor," I said. "My assistant resigned and I need a new one as soon as possible."

"I know, we've been working on that," the HR lady said.

I rolled my eyes. "In the meantime, could you please schedule a day off for me?" I asked. "And make lunch reservations for two at a restaurant followed by a mani-pedi." My day next month with Candy finally had a place on the calendar, and now I had to get ready for a simple lunch date with my official suitor, Chris. I had to figure out how to talk to him about adopting Anna's baby.

"So, I have the chance to go out with real estate tycoon, Ms. Leslie Ann Chancellor. How are you feeling?" Outside of Candy, Chris was the only one who knew my full name.

I smiled as I took a seat at one of my favorite Italian restaurants. "Better, thanks to my sweet friend, Christopher Paul Schaeffer." I gave him a quick wink under the dim lighting in the restaurant. The vintage space smelled of cilantro, grated cheese, and garlic, but I loved it. "Thank you for convincing me to take the afternoon off." I squinted to read the tiny font on the menu.

Chris looked at me with soft eyes, not the way he did years ago—eyes of deep concern, compassion, and care. I needed that, wanted it, really. I reached across the table and took his hand, remembering how much Chris had been there for me and how much I actually loved him too. He returned the squeeze and we exchanged warm smiles. We knew where this was going. And somehow, in my heart, I knew that going there didn't mean forgetting Rob. It was like Chris said, we were walking to the end of the road together, and I wouldn't be alone. I'd have someone to love again until we found whatever the end of the road looked like.

I slipped on my readers and tried to decide on something to eat. A tossed salad sounded good, but so did a bowl of warm, bisque soup.

"What did you want?" I asked Chris.

"I think I'll have their margarita pizza." Chris didn't surprise me with the simplicity of his order. "What are you thinking?"

"I think I'll have the bisque soup sans brandy or white wine," I said and reached for a complimentary piece of bruschetta. This restaurant always had exceptional hor d'oeuvres.

"How is Candy feeling about, you know...us?" Chris asked.

"She hasn't said much," I said. "Honestly, she hasn't been saying too much of anything lately." As I said the words, I thought a little harder about the last time Candy had mentioned my dating. She hadn't been singing around the house either, which worried me. *What about when we had a new little one in the house? Would she sing then?*

"Why haven't you guys had practice at the studio?" I asked Chris, pushing the baby topic to the side for a moment.

"Candy should have told you," Chris sighed.

"What?" I placed my bruschetta down on my plate.

"It needs to come from her," Chris said.

"Can you at least give me a hint?" I pressed him.

Chris handed the waitress the menu and leaned forward. "She loves you."

I stared at him. *What did I miss?* How did Chris surprise me when I intended to surprise him about the baby?

◆》 ・◆・ 《◆

"Candy?" I called when I got home.

Candy stood at the top of the steps with questioning eyes. Her curls escaped her messy bun on all sides and the creases in her hoodie indicated she'd been studying for longer than usual.

"Yeah," Candy said and came all the way down the steps.

146

"I miss hearing you sing," I said slowly, observing her movements.

She shifted her feet a little and didn't say anything. "I'm growin' up tomorrow." She sang the words from the song she shared with Rob. "I have SATs to study for now."

I squinted at her. "Gary from the county fairgrounds texted me on the way home and asked if you'd be willing to perform at the Honeybrook Hot Cocoa Festival."

She paused. I could tell she wanted to do it. "I don't know. I haven't practiced in a while."

"Can you let me know by the end of the week?" I asked her, taking off my blazer and draping it over one arm. "I think you'd do an amazing job."

She gave me a soft smile. "I kind of need to be here with family first." I caught her hidden meaning. She'd held back something from me, and my nerves had blinded me to it. She'd been offered the single and turned it down, hadn't she?

*With family?* She worried about me. My heart fell to the basement. I didn't know if I should be grateful she was safe or disappointed because of the missed opportunity. As I watched her trot back up the stairs, I wished I could show her the inside of my heart and how much I just wanted the absolute best of both worlds for her. I wanted her to live her dream, but I wanted her to be safe even more.

# Chapter 13: Candy

I SAT IN MY cold, metal chair in the school auditorium, waiting for Chris to come in for youth group. Scott saw me when he walked in and sat across from me, not next to me as usual. *Fine,* I thought. *Don't sit next to me.*

Chris walked in, coffee cup in one hand, teacher bag in the other. "All right guys, let's talk about how that Fruit of the Spirit challenge is coming along." He sat down next to me and gave me a slight head tilt. Why did he care about me and Scott? If anything, why wasn't he telling me I was exempt from the Fruit of the Spirit challenge yet? After everything Mom and I had been through, that was the least he could do.

"I'm trying to show joy," Scott said. "Mom doesn't have anyone else to show her a smile, so I want to give her one, you know?" Scott's voice came out rough. My heart sank. He's trying to show joy to Mrs. Carrington after his own dad died? My hands grew sweaty as guilt hit me. I met his gaze, and he quickly looked down. He should have been exempted too.

"Scott, if you can't find joy right now, we'd understand," Chris said in a low voice.

*Chris was letting Scott off the hook and not me? Even though he saw everything that happened at our house?* I stared down at my boots. *I shouldn't have to participate in this. I should be excused too. Even God would know that.*

❖❖ ·❖· ❖❖

As I sat on my bed with my phone, I realized I needed to apologize to Scott, even if I didn't want to. Even if I never wanted to make the single or I lost the youth group challenge since Chris wouldn't excuse me, I always wanted Scott to know I cared.

I let the phone tilt a little in my hand before I swiped it open and tapped the buttons to get to his contact info. I stared at his picture. Our picture. Our selfie reminded me of happier days when we were in the band, Mom didn't use oxygen, and Scott's dad was alive. The pre-fire days. I bit my lip as I pressed the call icon.

Scott answered immediately and my heart sped up. "Hello?""Hi, Scott?" I began.

"Yeah?"

"Um, I just wanted to go on the record for saying I'm sorry for being inconsiderate of your feelings. I really do care about you losing your dad."

Silence.

"It's hard, I know."

"Candy, I get it. Ms. Leslie is sick and you want to be there for her." Scott's voice came out low and caring.

Warmed by his forgiveness, I stood and went to the window, looking in the direction of his house, and let myself be open. "Mom scares me sometimes. Sometimes she's normal, and sometimes it's like I'm praying she'll be okay. She had a really rough go of it at the hospital, and I only had a prayer. I could only say a scared prayer."

"I get it," Scott said. "You chose to show love to your family, and love comes from God."

I took my phone off speaker and held it against my ear. "I'm still really sorry for not showing enough love to you and keeping your heart in mind."

"It's okay," he said. "I know we'll play again, even if it's not the single."

"Yeah," I told him. "Or something."

Our shared phrase elicited a much-needed laugh, and I let myself smile at the memories that flitted through my head. My hand ached for a microphone, but even more than that, my heart desperately wanted an alive and mostly healthy mom.

# Chapter 14: Leslie

"**S**O, SHE WANTED TO give up the single because she worried about me." I sank into the couch in the living room.

"It shows her maturity." Chris tried to comfort me, but I still felt awful. "She cares a lot about you, and she's not so selfish as to let music consume her."

"Chris, I'm not going to get better. Candy has her whole life in front of her," I moaned.

"You have your whole life too. COPD patients live long lives. You've had major changes recently, but you'll even out. I just have to put some more weight on you." And with that, Chris gave me a soft pinch on my side, and I laughed.

"I'd love something warm." I stood and walked to the kitchen. Chris followed. "It's so rainy out, I think it's the only way to take off the chill."

"What are you making?" Chris raised an eyebrow as I took out one of my many unused gadgets. Bessie, our former housekeeper, had used the rice maker a million times, but I never had.

"I think rice?" I held out the round machine. "It's just water and rice in here, right?"

"Just rice?" Chris asked and walked into the pantry, coming out with chicken broth and a can of soup. "How about we cook this rice in chicken broth and we mix it with some of the soup to thicken the soup up, okay?"

I looked at the vegetable soup. I guessed that would work. I was so cold, and I really just wanted something warm and soft. I turned on the rice cooker and took the broth from Chris.

"Do I pour in the whole thing?"

Chris laughed and gave me a peck on the cheek. "Why don't you heat up the soup? The can opener is in your middle drawer."

Feeling a little embarrassed by my lack of kitchen skills, I nodded and tried to follow his directions. I found the pot where I thought it should be and thankfully the automatic can opener didn't need a battery replacement. After almost half an hour, we had a warm meal, and I finally stopped feeling like I lived in the North Pole. I sat opposite Chris and took another savory bite. I might never know how to make anything that wasn't already cut or canned, but in that moment, eating a hot lunch with my best friend after everything I'd been through made me grateful for the simple joy of just that.

"How do you like it?" Chris asked.

"It's good, thank you," I said.

"Is this the first meal we've made as a couple?" Chris asked.

I felt myself go from warm to hot. "I guess so," I said and smiled at him. His smile back warmed me even more.

# Chapter 15: Candy

"**S**COTT," I SAID AS soon as he answered the phone. "Mom wants to know if we'd like to sing for the Hot Cocoa Festival here in Honeybrook."

Scott paused. "I thought you gave up on singing."

I flopped onto my bed and began to fidget with my hair. The single felt like a million miles away and so did my dreamy, almost-famous life. That corner of my heart felt like dried, crushed flowers, and it hurt to really think about it. But, Mom had suggested the local concert and the chance to sing again warmed me somehow.

Scott hesitated before saying, "I don't think Nina is going to be in town that week. And I don't think Nate is either."

"It doesn't have to be the whole band." I took one loose curl and twisted it slowly as I spoke. "Just you and me singing would be cool."

"Candy, you could sing about toothpaste and sound amazing," Scott said. "Wouldn't this only get your hopes up again?"

And with that, the tears splashed onto my phone screen. He was right. I'd walk right back to where my dreams both lived and died.

"Candy, are you there?" Scott asked.

I sniffled. "Scott, does God give us dreams just to wave them in our faces? Does He bring us out of dusty, country roads and let us taste a part of our dreams, then take the spoon out of our mouths?"

Scott remained quiet yet again before saying, "I serve the God Who finishes what He starts. I think He's not done with you yet."

I bit my lip to hold back more tears that threatened to fall. After fighting flames, I had hoped for my family more than fame. But this was nothing more than a talent show. The mayor wouldn't be mean to me and mom in front of everyone who voted for him, right?

"So, the Hot Cocoa Festival?" Scott asked.

I let out a long sigh. "Mom seemed okay with the concert and she's been doing better, so I guess so." I truly prayed to do the right thing. After all, I knew what my home was like. Scott didn't.

# Chapter 16: Leslie

I SIFTED THROUGH THE mail on the kitchen counter—nothing of importance. The newspaper fell open to the obituary section. Sam Rosewater died? Why hadn't the mayor said anything? My heart actually went out to the mayor. Of course, maybe Candy would be safe onstage now, especially with the Hot Cocoa Festival coming up.

My mind traveled back to an earlier meeting with the mayor and his threats for me to lose everything. I thought about the night I lost my own parents. They'd been everything that mattered. Now that Sam was gone, would Rosewater dig his heels in even deeper? I paced the kitchen, thinking about how my world had crumpled in one night in college. I had no control back then. I barely had any control now, unlike Dad who always had control.

Dad's work and gambling habits were something we didn't talk about often. I'd lost my own journals of half-finished ideas about what went on in my family. I had thought I knew why Dad had so many unusual "contacts," but those diaries were buried somewhere. I was sixteen then, and I'd had no real proof of any of my wild theories. Dad worked, traveled, and always bought me everything I ever wanted. Whenever he gambled, I assumed he always won. We always had money in cash.

Feeling nostalgic, I went upstairs to my old wooden chest–the one I took with me from my grandparent's house when I married Rob. It smelled of mothballs now. It seemed lonely all by itself in the guest bedroom, but I knew it had so many memories inside. I sat on the floor in the near-empty room wrestling with the half-baked ideas I grew up believing. Dad was in business. Mom never liked his traveling or his gambling, and he always told me that his business was 'top secret' so I couldn't ask him more questions. I'd journaled my way to four conclusions years ago. Dad worked as a government spy or agent. Or maybe he worked in the special forces in an unnamed project. Dad worked despite our money. What if Dad had a high-stress job he loved? There was also the dreaded idea that Dad did something shady and crossed the worst family that forgot nothing and sought revenge regardless of passed time.

Now, I opened the chest and took out the photo albums of my family.

I saw myself sporting a side ponytail for a high school yearbook picture. I fingered another Polaroid shot of my mother in the living room, legs crossed and wearing the flower dress she loved so much. Then there was a picture of Dad talking to a man that only seemed vaguely familiar. I lifted the book up to my nose, studying the man, and went numb. I had just seen that face yesterday. It was the mayor. Another picture showed Dad with Uncle Gio. He was an uncle in name only and had helped me move after my parents died. The dust from the old photos, Mom's old sweaters, and the like made me remember the sweet, innocent days of long ago. As I fingered the album, I accidentally loosened the plastic covering of one of the photos. The photo of Dad with the mayor slipped out, and so did a folded piece of notebook paper. I opened it.

*My dearest, if you're reading this note, I'm dead now. I'm sorry it worked out this way. Know that I'm proud of you and I know that your grandparents will take care of you. I learned late that if you choose peace, you'll get peace. If you choose justice, you'll get justice. Sometimes in life, you won't get both. You were my princess, a true little light in my dark world and you were worth fighting for.*

I started crying as I read my Dad's scrawled handwriting and imagined his heavy southern accent that I could easily achieve.

*But the mayor told me that he'd haunt every living family member of mine until he died. It wasn't your fault that Sam Rosewater lost the game. Remember that. I won the land fair and square. Jeremy was never your fault, but what Jeremy did to you was unforgivable in my book. Leslie, darling, if you are reading this, don't let them scare you. I've made sure you have everything you need. You may have gotten married now, but you still have fighting St. John blood in your veins. You've got this.*

*Until Heaven,*

*Dad*

Hot tears ran down my face as I considered the threat. The mayor wanted me, and he would soon make a move to hurt Candy. Like I thought, he had something to do with my mom and dad's deaths. My heart ached for my teen journals. They might have given me more to go by.

I thought about how Rob and I had written letters to Candy for her to open when she turned eighteen. Maybe Candy would want to read Rob's letter now. I ran my fingers through my hair and tried to ground my thoughts. I flipped through some more relics and took out a soft cream sweater with tiny flowers that belonged to my mother. Under it were some crumpled postcards. I picked them up and scanned them briefly. The handwriting on the first danced across the tiny rectangle in huge, illustrious letters. It said, *"Oliver. Don't worry. We'll take care of those rich people who think they own the whole town. −Sam."*

*The mayor and his brother retaliated and had my parents killed?! Assuming that's who "those rich people" were.* I tilted the lid of the chest which had been hastily given to me. I'd never searched it like this before. I'd lived the life of a college student, a grad student, a married woman, mom, and now a single parent and widow. Before today, the bottom of an old chest didn't matter. What did Dad mean by 'everything I needed?' Money? Success?

I scanned another postcard. It was a love note from my mom to my dad on one of his trips. I sat up straighter when I read it. It seemed like my mom hadn't felt safe at home either. It read: *"My dearest, I don't feel safe here after knowing how you got the land this weekend. The Rosewater brothers have been by our house, asking a lot of questions. Concerning ones. Please come home."* I smoothed the postcard down. It seemed like I had accidentally stumbled across actual proof that the Rosewaters had been after us, but what could I do with it? It would only prove my dad was in the wrong too. I was still sitting there, wondering what my dad had done for a living and whether he was more innocent than he seemed, when Candy's voice from the doorway made me jump.

"Mom?" Candy walked into the room.

I shook my head at her and closed the photo album.

Candy looked at me with widened eyes and sat down beside me.

"Mayor Rosewater threatened to hurt me, but a long time ago he vowed to hurt our whole family."

"Why?"

I reached for a tissue in my pocket and wiped my nose. "Well, there's something you need to know."

# Chapter 17: Candy

O F ALL THE TIMES in the world for my mom to tell me that we've always had a family feud, she chose this moment. Who knew that the mayor had a late brother who organized country music concerts? Why didn't anyone tell me these things? Mom placed napkins on the table and gave me a firm look.

"Chris is coming over for dinner." She sat a bowl of bread rolls on the table. "Let's not talk about it, okay?"

"Did Daddy know?" I ignored her request and flopped into a seat at the table.

"Yes, Dad knew all about the tension between my family and the Rosewaters," Mom admitted. "But Chris only knows the basics."

I reached for a bread roll and started eating, thinking about how the mayor could possibly find it okay to try to ruin my fledging career. I'd read the letter. He wanted to get rid of all St. Johns. In theory, that included me–a girl who secretly dreamed of being in front of the camera, one of the easiest targets in the world. But if I claimed to have faith, why didn't I feel brave enough to stay and not be afraid of anything?

I wanted to run and admit that Mom was right. It wasn't safe onstage. Mom was too sick for me to leave her. I swallowed hard. Maybe I shouldn't sing for YouTube either.

Maybe. But how would that keep me and Mom safe? And how could *I* keep us safe?

# Chapter 18: Leslie

"CHRIS, IF I ACCEPT Jesus, will the panic attacks go away?" I sat down on the couch, holding hot tea. We'd had the quietest of Valentine's Day celebrations: a warm lunch I'd treated him to at his favorite restaurant, and he'd given me an embarrassing number of flowers.

Chris looked at me with soft eyes. "If you accept Jesus, you will have Him as your Lord and Savior. You will be promised eternity in Heaven and forgiveness of all your sins."

I looked down, wishing that once and for all my nerves would be cured.

"I know it's been a long time," Chris said slowly. "I can't begin to imagine what it's like to not have full control of your emotions."

I laced my fingers together on my lap. Chris and Rob had both witnessed the onset of my anxiety. Now, struggling with COPD only made it worse. I never knew when I'd struggle to breathe or when the disease would get worse. Or if it did, would Candy and I have what it takes to keep it together?

"Candy's heart is for Jesus," I said in a low tone. "Her heart sings for Him."

Chris nodded.

Tears gathered around my eyelashes. I thought of seeing my angel babies again in Heaven, along with Rob, my parents, and even my grandparents. After all, Dad had promised 'until Heaven.' My heart broke open. I wanted that now. "Even if God doesn't heal me on this side of Heaven..." I let the tears fall. "And even if life continues to throw curveballs," I whispered, voice trembling as Chris moved closer to me. A true yearning for Christ filled me. "I want to hold His Hand."

Chris hugged me and a warmth came over me that I didn't expect--a soothing freedom. I didn't expect to instantly breathe better, but a sense of assurance flooded me as I prayed the salvation prayer with Chris. Somehow, I knew that the next time panic struck me, the Hand of God would walk me through to the other side. I had that now.

"Welcome to the family." Chris smiled at me.

*The family*, I thought. *Funny how one father got me into this huge mess and my new Heavenly Father is going to walk me out of it. Two very different families indeed.*

"Thank you." I sniffled Chris and I sat together in silence for a while as I let the sweet new peace sit on my heart.

# Chapter 19: Candy

"FLOWERS?" I BLINKED AT the bouquet Scott handed me at lunch. Nina glanced at me, then quickly walked away. So much for second chances and us staying friends despite the single.

"Well, it's Valentine's Day. I wanted to get my girl a gift or something." Scott gave me his sweet grin that showed off his dimple. I hadn't forgotten. I reached into my bookbag and handed him a bar of chocolate I'd picked out on a long walk home from school one day. I'd wrapped it with red paper and a huge white bow.

"Happy Valentine's Day, Scott," I said.

"Happy Valentine's Day." Scott leaned across the cafeteria table and whispered, "Look in your bouquet."

I reached into my bouquet of flowers and read the card. "In a world full of sadness, burned rubble and destruction, you are the one flower that brightens my life." I grew warm.

"Thank you." I smiled at him and reached for one of his tater tots.

"You're the best." Scott winked at me. I squeezed his hand. His eyes caught my heart and I knew I would have to be honest with him. In a low whisper, so our classmates wouldn't hear, I told him the updates on my family history as we popped ketchup-drenched tater tots. The boy I loved needed to know about my family secrets. If I couldn't tell Scott, who else could I trust? I had no regrets.

"It's like having a modern-day family feud," I whined.

Scott placed one hand over mine as he moved closer to me. "That's deep. But Candy, I'm glad you're safe now."

"Me too," I said, taking my tray to the trashcan.

After lunch in the noisy cafeteria, we walked to class slowly, letting the warmness of our shared moment sink in a little more. Before we parted ways, Scott walked over to my classroom door and leaned against the wall.

"Well?"

I looked away for fear of the eyes of the students and possibly teachers.

Scott moved closer and our eyes met. Without thinking, we gave each other the softest, sweetest Valentine's Day kiss.

# Chapter 20: Candy

"CANDY, HOLD UP." CHRIS stopped me before I left for the day. He hung up his phone call and shoved his phone in his pocket. I stepped closer to him as people leaving for the day passed us.

"What's wrong?" I adjusted my backpack and glanced around for Scott.

"If God opened another door for you to sing that wouldn't hurt your mom, would you walk through it?" Chris asked.

I pulled back and looked at him. "Of course, why?"

"The Fruit of the Spirit is love, joy, peace, patience, kindness, goodness, faithfulness, gentleness, and self-control," Chris quoted. "I've seen a lot of love from you, a lot of kindness and goodness too. Stay on the lookout for blessings when you honor God, okay?"

Surprised, I just nodded. What did Chris mean? I juggled the thoughts in my head, feeling as if I could never get everything right, even though I desperately wanted to.

"Chris?" I didn't expect my voice to sound like a mouse. "How do I know if I'm doing enough?" I asked.

"God decides that," Chris said in a low voice as we walked outside and into the crowded parking lot. "Serve God with all your heart. You've made the right decisions, but God cares about our dreams, so be open to changes in what we think are 'our plans'." Chris used air quotes. "He'll take care of the rest." He reached back into his pocket and began texting someone.

I gave him a hopeful glance. I wished I knew what "the rest" looked like.

◆》— ◆ ◆ — 《◆

"Green!" I exclaimed when I ran inside the house and immediately hugged Mom. Maybe putting music aside was the trick, and it actually helped me a little too. After all, I'd need decent SAT scores to get into the family college or any local college that would keep me close to Mom.

Mom laughed her signature laugh. "On the practice SATs?"

"Yes!" I smiled at her as she stood by the sink. Mom held me a little longer than usual, and I knew she was proud of me.

Seeing Mom the way I remembered her before we lost Daddy made me happy—sober, laughing, and cheering me on in my school work like years ago. And even though she was dating Chris, it didn't bother me in the least.

# Chapter 21: Leslie

I T WARMED MY HEART that Candy agreed to sing at the local winter carnival. I took a seat in a foldout chair and wrapped a scarf over my nose, waiting for the concert to begin. I wondered what she'd sing since I really hadn't heard much from my little songbird. I mean, I'd suggested the performance since it was a tiny event with security, and I figured Rosewater wouldn't pull off anything crazy in front of his constituents, but my little girl seemed a bit off these days. Maybe she was okay with being a local sweetheart. I settled into my chair and began clapping as she walked out wearing her ruffled dress and boots.

"This song is new," she began. "I hope y'all like it."

Are you listenin' from Heaven/

Can you hear me now/

I'm playin' music still/

Like you showed me how/

Are you listenin' from Heaven/

I guess the songs have changed/

We don't sing our duet now/

But my love hasn't gone away/

It's been years since I said goodbye, but it feels like yesterday/

I thought that I'd feel better now, but the pain won't go away/

I've learned to live with what feels like a fraction of my heart/

But that ain't really true, cuz' Jesus holds both our hearts.

A lump caught in my throat as I watched her hold the mic to her mouth and sing with a passion I hadn't noticed before. Scott walked out onstage and joined her.

Are you listenin' from Heaven/

Can you hear us now/

Scott sang and Candy left her stool to join him.

I know that both of you are listenin' from up above/

And I know that death doesn't ever separate love/

The two harmonized beautifully and despite Candy having written a song about Rob before, something about this song sounded different, maybe because it represented both Rob and Drew? Scott wrapped one arm around her waist as they ended the song.

Singin' about our Daddies/

Wish you were here right now/

Singin' about the old times/

How we'd make you both proud/

We all have 'em/

Those good ol' days/

Mine include Daddy/

Even though he's gone away/

Candy lowered her head and her cowgirl hat hid her face from the crowd.

Are you listenin' from Heaven... She closed out the song and strummed her guitar with a soft stroke of what I couldn't really describe other than love, and the audience roared. They'd always cheered her on, but tonight, her voice had been so clear, so powerful, that the emcee asked her and Scott to keep singing. Candy's face took on the expression I felt at the office—it was her second home.

She and Scott both got back on their stools and sang.
What don't you like about winter/
It's freezin' cold/
You gotta walk around like you're eighty years old/
In seventeen sweaters/
Six pairs of socks/
And eatin' hot cereal like you're Goldilocks/
What's not to like about winter?

The crowd laughed, then started to clap. Candy's energetic yet relaxed comfort onstage and how she worked with the crowd made me realize that she needed more than Honeybrook. My heart knew that my daughter's voice was stronger than Honeybrook. And despite the alarm bells of anxiety that kept going off in my head, I knew that she'd been called for more, made for more and I couldn't hold her back. I'd have to let her know she should walk into the studio again. She should never have given it up.

The two finished with *Amazing Grace*, then bowed as they walked offstage.

"I feel like I've been treated to a celebrity concert," the emcee said, still clapping.

*I think you were,* I thought and searched for the dynamic duo that pulled off an incredible performance without even trying.

# Chapter 22: Candy

**M**Y PHONE RANG THE next day with an unknown number. I swiveled around in my chair upstairs and watched it buzz a little on my desk. Expecting a weird spam caller, I hesitated to answer it, but I did.

"Hello?"

At that precise moment, Mom walked in and sat on my bed, her hair damp but tied into a messy bun. I turned the phone on speaker.

"Is this Candy Chancellor?" The man's voice sounded familiar.

"Yes."

"This is Grayson Lee. Your manager gave me your number."

I froze. Grayson Lee? Mom looked as surprised as me.

"Chris told me that you turned down the single because your mom was ill."

Mom's eyes widened. She placed one hand over her chest and stared into my heart. Her eyes held an electric charge and she stared at me with the same boardroom passion she expressed right before she sank her teeth into a big deal. Did she think I missed a chance? She wasn't mad at me for giving it up, right? The timing for the single was wrong. She'd been so sick, like big-deal sick.

Tears formed in my eyes as memories of what seemed like a lifetime ago played in my mind–Mom before she needed oxygen, before all this.

"Grace Unchained rescinded their offer," I managed to say through the frog in my throat.

"I heard." Grayson's British-accented voice carried a warmth I didn't expect. "But I wanted to let you know that I would have done the same exact thing for my mom. I would choose my family each time."

I placed the phone on the table and buried my head in my hands. Mom left my bed and sat on the floor next to me in my chair. She closed her eyes and rubbed my back softly. I'd made the right choice for once?

"And sometimes, when we make right choices that don't always feel amazing to us, God shows us how He's working everything out for His glory."

I was sure he could hear me sniffling, but I tried to cover it up by clearing my throat.

"My record label, Born Again Records, heard about your story and I had a conversation with Chris. We'd love to produce two songs with you. We'd like to feature you in our next song, and we'd like to offer you a single," he said. "Provided that you let us record at your studio where your mom is okay with it."

I glanced at Mom and she nodded firmly, tears brimming in her eyes.

My heart started to race and I could feel it pounding in my ears.

"Oh my gosh! Thank you! Yes!" I squealed. "A thousand times, yes!"

Grayson Lee laughed. "We don't want to lose a voice nor a passionate praise like yours. I'll work out the details on my end and get back to you." And with that, he hung up and I leaned back in my chair shocked.

"Mom!!"

"I know!" Mom laughed and hugged me. "Congratulations, sweetie. You earned it."

I didn't feel like I'd earned it. I felt like I'd finally won an entire battle, and I'd been blessed with the one thing I'd been chasing and fighting for. A single. I had gotten one more chance, and it was even better than before. God had given me double–a feature and a single. The win tasted sweeter than the first time in New York because now I'd fought against all the obstacles in my way with the love of God and won.

"We get a feature and you actually want to make the single?" Scott asked me at the urgent band practice Chris had called. I didn't think anyone would show up after I'd shut everyone off over the last few weeks, but he showed. Surprisingly Nina and Nate did too. And they were holding hands when they came in.

"Yeah, if you guys want to," I said softly as we all sat in a circle on the floor. "Mom came first."

"Is your mom okay with this?" Nina's voice carried hesitation.

"Definitely." I smiled at her. "We're making the songs here."

Chris pushed the door open a little more to let Mom in. She seemed a little winded from climbing three flights of steps.

"And I'm more than okay with it." Mom sat down in the chair across from the piano and let out a long sigh. "You guys have talent. I wanted to overlook it as a hobby, but

I didn't see, well, as my late husband would have put it, 'your dream or calling.'"

Chris gave Mom a quick glance, but then ran his fingers through his hair. "I think Rob would have thought exactly that, and I'd have to agree with him." I appreciated Chris remembering Daddy too in this beautiful moment—the moment where Mom saw us for who we were and who were called to be: singers for Christ.

I didn't know I had a twisted knot in my heart from locking up my dreams, but as Scott handed me my guitar, Nate took his spot on the drums, and Nina took her seat at the piano, the knot came undone. Despite it being a dark February night, my heart soared and sang as if it were a warm summer day—just like the balmy day Daddy and I shared years ago on the beach as the sun set. I sang, letting every single note reach for Heaven, laying my worship at the feet of Jesus. New words poured from my soul.

Did you ever just want to give up/
Did you ever feel just stuck/
Did you ever feel like you could never grow?
God's the Gardener/
He tends to our hearts/
God's the Gardener/
He sees past our faults/
God's the Gardener/
He has plans for us/
To grow/
So don't give up now/
You're not stuck, you're growing/
Don't give up/
You're right where you should be/
Don't stop/
Don't give in/
Keep your head up/

Keep believin'/
In God the Gardener

I put the mic back in the holder and caught Nina staring at me. Scott held his gaze on me too, and I worried I'd been too confident. "How does that sound?" I asked.

"I think it sounds amazing!" Scott said and came to give me a hug. He'd kept up on the guitar, but Nina had started writing the lyrics down.

Chris smiled at me softly. "I know it's very last minute, but do you guys think you can perfect this song for the single?"

We agreed only if we could nail it a second time. We surprised ourselves with the way the song came out. The pureness, the authenticity, and the joy radiated throughout the room as we practiced it again. No one could miss the power behind it. As Nina picked up the tune and ended the song with the last final notes of the piano, I caught Mom wiping a stray tear from her eye.

"Don't you ever stop," she said. "That was beautiful."

It was an award-winning statement coming from my mom, who could either take it or leave it when it came to music. Tonight, that was all that mattered.

# Chapter 23: Leslie

"**S**HE'S NOT GOING TO see me like she used to," I complained to Chris on the phone the next morning. "I didn't tell her my dad's real role in everything, and she only thinks my anxiety is based on losing her grandparents and siblings." I put my phone on speaker and placed it on the desk in my office. I needed meetings today with all of my departments about this land.

"Well, that's when you were diagnosed," Chris reminded me.

"Yeah, and that's when it was at its worst," I agreed. I slid one finger over my laptop and said nothing for a moment.

"Do you want her to know the real story?" Chris asked.

"Now that I don't know if Rosewater is going to kill me, maybe I should," I sighed. I didn't believe in sharing everything with Candy, especially not my dark past. Sweet stories about her grandparents were one thing and so were family traditions, but never did I want to tell her the painful memories that I now unpacked in therapy. Those were a catalyst. After Chris hung up and I got ready for all my video chats, I wondered which story would convey everything in the most succinct, appropriate way. After all, I was a believer now, so God would help me, that I knew.

Mike entered the chat first. "Leslie."

I knew he would never use the professional "Ms." in front of my name like the entire office. I'd corrected him at least twice while Rob was living, and he chose to ignore it. Now, it irked me even more.

"We have other options for the Willis farm," Mike continued. "I know we don't build commercial, but what about homeless shelters?"

"Mike," I groaned. "If the mayor won't approve affordable housing in the middle of Honeybrook, what makes you think he'll approve homeless shelters?"

"Hear me out," Mike said. "We also build a drug rehab hospital on the premises and say that we want to heal Honeybrook."

I thought about how my own rehab center had been just outside of Honeybrook, but close enough to Honeybrook Hospital. People needed larger, more affordable facilities. My expenses for my month-long stay had been enormous. But I didn't build commercial facilities, and I really didn't want to expand that far, at least not yet while still trying to fill Rob's role and maintain mine.

Wendy joined the chat. "How is the plan for the Willis farmland purchase coming?"

"We still can't decide," Mike answered for me and I bristled. "We don't want to lose the money."

"We're still ironing out details." I didn't tell the team I had full plans of steam plowing ahead, not yet anyway.

Only the daily video chats with each of my teams maintained my sanity. Anxiety filled me at home. I was completely alone, and being on live video calls was the only way I could calmly work with people. I scheduled follow up calls for the next morning to ensure more of the same. I only had fifteen minutes for lunch before I turned on talk radio for the two and a half hours I had to work on my own paperwork and reply to emails.

My most important email made my hands shake.

*Dear Mayor Rosewater,*

*Outpricing humans who are working hard to put a roof over their heads isn't just immoral, but it should be illegal. After interviewing people experiencing homelessness, I learned that several people worked more than one job, but still couldn't afford an apartment payment.*

For a brief moment, I wanted a strong drink, but I pushed the feeling away.

*I understand that you are against affordable housing in the middle of Honeybrook, but as a builder, I can't see myself putting multi-million dollar homes there either. Honeybrook is a warm, welcoming town, and I'd like to see it kept that way. As mayor, your power should be used for good. I've been reflecting on our differences lately, and with all due respect, at our next meeting I expect to reach a compromise.*

A quick feeling of confidence shot through me as I thought about how I now had evidence on my side because of the postcards. Nothing bulletproof, but just enough edge.

I pressed send, then ran my fingers through my hair. It was my best shot.

# Chapter 24: Candy

"WE ALL HAVE ENEMIES," Mayor Rosewater said on the news that night while Mom and I ate dinner in the living room instead of the kitchen. "But listen, Violet. As mayor, I take care of my enemies, as we all should." Mom turned pale as we kept watching. The mayor looked right into the camera, right at me and Mom. Mom pinched the bridge of her nose and stopped eating. *How deep was this family feud?*

I ran upstairs to find the dusty photo album in the spare room. Mom hadn't done much with it since she found the note.

*What if...* I thought and reached for the note inside the chest. I read over the note again, this time using the gift of music God gave me, and let tunes flow through my head. *My dearest, if you're reading this note, I'm dead now. I'm sorry it worked out this way. Know that I'm proud of you and I know that your grandparents will take care of you. I learned late that if you choose peace, you'll get peace. If you choose justice, you'll get justice. Sometimes in life, you won't get both.*

I scanned through the rest of the letter until I got to the closing, *Until Heaven, Dad.*

I reached for my phone in my pocket and texted Scott. **What does a song about peace and justice look like? Write it and I'll play it. Why?**

I wanted to throw shade at the mayor, and I needed to let out my feelings about how he kept trying to scare me and mom. I switched apps on my phone and started typing away.

I don't know where you got your spunk/

But it blazes like fire in your eyes/

So, honey, please know that there's only a fight worth fighting for if there's a prize/

Until Heaven I'll hold you/

'Til Heaven I'll protect you/

'Til Heaven I'll be daddy and you'll be darlin' to me/

Those words made me think of my own daddy and my eyes stung a little. Couldn't I tell on the mayor without telling on the mayor? Would someone outside of Honeybrook even comment? I didn't want the mayor to see it, but I needed the song to exist—to let the world know we couldn't be completely silenced.

Peace is a choice/

Justice is a reward/

I picked the one that made me wield a sword/

Don't ever think I lost/

My heart beats with you/

If you're readin' this letter/

Life treated you better/

And our family didn't die with me/

Until Heaven I'll hold you...

I kept tapping out the chorus until Mom walked in.

"Honey, what are you doing with this old note from Grandpa?" Mom sat down next to me.

"Mayor Rosewater is really threatening us!" I exclaimed.

Mom softly rubbed my back. "Maybe he is and it's wrong, but in this case, there's some heat involved between me and the mayor at my work right now—like helping out neighbors with their affordable housing. I need him to sign off on that."

I looked at Mom. She was going to be threatened because she wanted to help others?

Mom seemed to catch on to what I was thinking since she added, "It's going to be the price of doing business."

Somehow that sounded wrong. Practiced, but wrong.

Later that night, I strummed my guitar on my bed and began singing my new song about the mayor's unfairness. I set up my camera just in case it was good enough for the internet.

"This song is dedicated to every daddy that left too soon, to every daddy who fights for his family, and to every daddy out there who has the heart of a lion. We heard your battle cry. May justice roar, freedom ring, and may peace reign again." I practiced my dedication and began to sing *Until Heaven*...

I uploaded the video and included the hashtag **#honeybrookproblems**.

# Chapter 25: Candy

"**W**HY CAN'T YOU REST home alone, Mom?" I asked later that night once Chris had gone home after a warm dinner of meatballs and spaghetti. Now, I sat on top of her bed and reached over to click on the lamp on her nightstand.

"What do you mean, honey?" Mom asked, propping herself up with more pillows.

"I mean, if you don't mind me asking, why are you against being home alone?"

Mom turned a crimson red and looked away from me. "Health reasons, honey." She closed her journal. "The Carringtons are nice people, aren't they?" The conversation shift rocked me.

"Of course." I thought of my dear, sweet Scott and how I wanted to text him sweet dreams before I turned in.

"Chris is a lovely person," Mom continued. "So are the people who work at Chancellor Homes, your teachers, and even the Andersons. Only Tommy made the dreadful mistake."

I looked at Mom carefully. Was she going to answer my question?

"As you know, the Rosewaters and my family didn't get along very well." Mom tossed the remote around in her hand softly, as if she wasn't sure if she was going to continue. "You know how Mayor Rosewater threatened to eliminate the St. Johns?" Mom asked.

I nodded. I still couldn't believe he would threaten to do that over land.

Mom didn't meet my eyes. "Well, grandpa eliminated someone first."

At first, I didn't understand what she was saying. My sweet grandpa, who she said would have adored me? HE had killed someone? I blinked. "What?"

"I was about your age at one of our family's house parties in the early '90s. Mom and Dad left to talk to Uncle Gio." Mom gripped the remote so hard, I thought she'd actually crush it. "Jeremy Rosewater showed up. He was more of a party crasher, really." Tears started running down Mom's face. "We exchanged some unkind words I wish I never said." She wiped under her eyes. "But we were both underage drinking, and Jeremy got drunk. He came out of the house back into the yard, shouting my name. He beat–" Mom paused and rubbed her arm. "My ribs were broken and I had dozens of bruises. My dress was ruined." She kept her eyes down. "When your grandmother saw me, she nearly fainted. Dad promised me he'd handle it." Her voice grew softer. "I'll always blame myself for everything that happened after that."

"What happened?" I leaned forward on a throw pillow.

"When I came home from the hospital, my ribs were wrapped up, but my dad looked as if justice were served. He'd told me he'd taken care of everything. The next month, Jeremy died in a freak car accident. Allegedly, he ran his car off the bridge leaving Honeybrook into Ridge Creek. There was no police investigation, and it was deemed a complete accident. I didn't know Dad would go that far. I didn't say anything for a week. The Rosewaters said nothing either. It was all unspoken."

I moved closer to Mom on the bed. "Mom, I'm sorry! How was any of that your fault?"

"Your grandfather said he'd take care of it." Mom rested her head in her hand, a piece of tubing caught between her fingers. "He had Jeremy killed, but I insulted Jeremy, his family, egged him on that night, and asked for him to be sent away."

I went numb.

"I've always had question marks about what Dad and Jeremy did together, but I still felt like I most certainly tipped Dad over the edge to take such a drastic action." At this, Mom reached for her glass of water. "The mayor retaliated almost a year later with Mom and Dad's freak boating accident. And now that your dad isn't here to be a buffer, he wants to finish the job for good. I always knew that he would get me if he had the chance. He knows Jeremy wouldn't have hurt me if I hadn't done something or said something." She sniffled. "And he's right."

"Was Daddy at the party?" I asked, blinking fast as I tried to take in all the information.

"No, but like I told you before, your dad knew part of the story in college and the whole story when we were married. I unraveled at home alone, so much so that I had to go to the hospital." Mom returned her glass of water to the night stand. "It was a nervous breakdown. I'd never experienced that level of anxiety in my life. Your dad and I tried having me stay home alone one more time, but it was the same outcome. We promised never again." Her face grew even more sober. "The mayor knows I know this story, which is why I'm sure he'll stop at nothing to destroy me now that your father's gone." Mom readjusted her pillows. "Your grandfather may have had the wrong idea on how to fix things, but your dad and I built Chancellor Homes and we always prided ourselves on delivering happily-ever-afters the right way. The mayor won't destroy it." Mom slid on her glasses and clicked on the television. "I'll fight him to the ground if I have to."

I didn't expect this from Mom. I couldn't imagine her as a saucy teenager, provoking Jeremy Rosewater into hostility. No one expects that from their mom. I didn't even know if I was glad that my unknown grandpa "took care" of Jeremy or not. Killing was wrong, but Jeremy legitimately hurt my mother and scarred her for life. I looked at her, remembering her last panic attack. She'd developed severe anxiety from that night. Guilt for being upset at Mom's anxiety consumed me. It wasn't even her fault. She just carried it like it was. We both had trauma as teens, but she developed anxiety as a result of hers. My heart gave way to compassion and I let out a slow sigh.

"I'm not going to sleep," Mom sighed. "If you need me, I'll be in the guestroom working on the renovation logistics." Mom rolled out of bed and began pushing her oxygen tank out of the room. I helped her. It was huge and too big to take downstairs. The downstairs tank would have to be rolled a long way to her home office, but with both of us, we could definitely set this one up in the other room down the hallway. Mom thanked me and kissed me on the head.

"Sweet dreams, honey. If you learned anything tonight, don't solve your problems with smoking and liquor." Mom took a seat in the huge chair and looked over her glasses at me. "And don't seek revenge. Two wrongs are just that: two wrongs."

My heart sank a little as I nodded, then left to brush my teeth and get ready for bed myself. The warm amber light across the hallway meant that Mom wasn't recovering well, wasn't resting, and still couldn't sleep. The rustling across the hall lasted all night.

I know I slept, but Mom emerged from her makeshift home office looking exhausted. "It's finally day," she sighed. "I can start video calls in an hour."

So that was how Mom felt connected to the outside world and not home alone during work hours. I grabbed a banana from the bowl on the counter.

"I have six scheduled for the day, so I need to freshen up." Mom hugged me. "We want to get the land in both Maryland and Virginia if we have the resources."

"Okay." I went to grab my backpack. I wanted Scott to hear my guitar solo and hoped he wouldn't be too mad I posted without him. I thought I did a pretty good job... until the mayor found my YouTube video and messaged Mom about it.

"I will have both of you!" I heard Mayor Rosewater's unmistakable voice on speaker as soon as I got home. Mom paced the kitchen floor, nodding.

"What does your daughter think she's doing posting a song like that online?" Mayor Rosewater clearly had found the one and only YouTube video I sort of didn't want him to see. It was for Grandpa, Grandma and Honeybrook, not him.

"I don't know what you're talking about." Mom stared at me and my knees grew wobbly. I swung my backpack off my shoulders, growing angry that my grandparents couldn't even be memorialized in a tiny online video.

"Get this, Leslie. I always take care of my enemies." He hung up and Mom stared at me.

"Candy, why did you post a song about grandpa?" Mom stood in the middle of the kitchen. "I told you that leaving things alone was the price of doing business. Now the mayor thinks we're threatening him because, well, he doesn't take kindly to us using words like justice and swords."

"But Mom, the mayor threatened you and killed grandma and grandpa," I said. I knew the full story now and would defend my choices.

"I can't do this." Mom wiped her hands on a kitchen towel and sank into a chair at the table. "God, help me," she whispered. She cupped her hands around her nose and mouth and drew in a deep breath. Dinner had been take-out, but Chris promised to come over afterwards for a movie.

"The mayor has no doubts now that I'm the only one with any possible documents." Mom gripped the edges of the table.

I hadn't thought about that. I'd been frustrated about what happened. The doorbell rang, and I left to answer it. It was Chris just in the nick of time since it was completely my fault that mom started having a scary panic attack. Even I was shaken up.

"Breathe, Leslie." Chris tossed his jacket on the floor. "Whatever it is, we can handle it, okay?"

Mom's hands shook and her face lost all color. "Rose-water thinks I'm going to go after him," she managed to say before she started crying.

"What?" Chris asked, blinking at me in confusion.

"Candy didn't mean it." Mom's breathing turned hurried. "I just have to prove that–" she started gasping and choking on air, and Chris moved closer to her with the trash can.

"Leslie, try to find something yellow in the room," Chris guided her. "Can you find three objects in the room?"

186

Mom turned a chalky gray and reached for the trash can. Her hands were still shaking and sweat ran down her face. Chris and I listened for the distinct catch as Mom began to hold her breath.

"Leslie, breathe out." He started to sound concerned. "Through your nose."

"He could kill us!" Mom squeaked and leaned forward on the table.

I walked over to her and gave her a tight squeeze. "Mom, the mayor won't get off with murder. It'll be okay. We just have to trust Jesus."

Chris started to rub Mom's back. "Breathe out."

Mom said nothing for a moment, but then her breathing returned, erratic. "Chris, I can't–" She closed her eyes.

In one quick motion, she held the trash can close to her face. I sighed as she lost her dinner in waves.

Chris placed a worried hand on Mom's back. "Woah." He held Mom's hair back and took the trash can. "You can't have anything left except your actual insides."

"We might lose everything." Her words echoed through the room.

Up until that moment, I thought I'd done the right thing, but as Mom gripped Chris by the shirt, I questioned everything. Mom didn't let go but lowered her head, seemingly aware and ashamed of the moment, yet in so much pain at the same time. Chris let her cry for a few minutes, then offered her medication. Mom turned it down and cried until she went hoarse. I heard her whispering tiny, almost incoherent prayers, which I knew was new for her. Chris moved closer to her and prayed with her. My shoulders slumped, and I didn't quite know where to stand in the darkened room. I couldn't undo any of this. Chris pulled Mom into a tight hug and thankfully Mom had worn herself out and had slowed down some. The tears had subsided, but the shakiness still remained.

Then, Chris did something Daddy did. He stood and picked Mom up, sat her on his lap and distracted her just enough so she would regain her footing. Then she fell asleep.

"Are you going to tell me why you posted a video trying to convict the mayor?" Chris raised an eyebrow at me.

Now my eyes grew misty.

"I wanted justice." As soon as I spoke, Mom stirred.

"Oh, my stomach." Mom groaned and blinked at us. "I'm sorry. I must have dozed off."

"Honey, you need to rest." Chris steadied Mom with one hand as she stood from his lap and we guided her to the living room couch. "Did you want toast and tea before you go to bed?"

Mom shook her head "no," but Chris sat down next to her. "It's burning," Mom muttered. She numbly reached for antacids that were awkwardly spilled on the living room table, but then turned back to Chris and sobbed herself back to sleep again.

"Your mom wanted it to be over with the Rosewaters," Chris told me firmly.

"And let him off with murder?" I asked, leaving my spot in the kitchen and joining him and Mom in the living room.

"Take a look at your mom," Chris said pointedly. Mom looked pained even in her sleep. One arm rested over her stomach and her breathing sounded more like panting than resting. "I have to help her go to bed, connect her to oxygen, and hopefully she won't freak out in the middle of the night. I understand wanting justice, Candy, but your mom is right. Some things are best settled face to face, not face to computer."

Mom's stomach bothered her so much that we couldn't get her to go up the steps. We used her downstairs oxygen, and Chris sat up across from her to monitor her breathing. I couldn't sleep either, especially after Mom started reliving the night with Jeremy Rosewater.

"Jeremy, please don't." She tossed and turned telling him to stop. Mom started fighting the air and my heart started to race. Chris's troubled expression matched my own thoughts.

"No!" Mom shrieked and my heart shattered.

# Chapter 26: Candy

"**I**T'S NOT ALL YOUR fault," Chris told me in the kitchen the next morning. I didn't believe him. I thought I'd used my gifts for good–fighting for justice and helping my family. Turns out I placed Mom on a sick day from work, and she still struggled to keep breakfast down. She softly kicked at the trashcan next to her and ate slowly, but didn't finish the small container of applesauce Chris offered her. I sat down at the table with her, hoping that would encourage her to eat.

"You need to eat something, Leslie," Chris said. "Did you want me to add cinnamon?"

Mom shook her head no.

Chris rubbed Mom on the back and she pushed the half-eaten applesauce away. Mom's face carried so much pain, I knew breakfast wasn't going to happen. Chris took the day off to keep her company, but I knew they had more going on. I sort of thought that Mom would eventually marry Chris since he spent so much time at our house, but neither one of them ever said anything. With the new drama I caused, I didn't even know if they'd ever tell me anything important again.

Sitting in the cafeteria that afternoon, I scrolled through social media and posted about the new single with Born Again Records. Taking a bite of grilled cheese,

I searched for the right picture to add. Now that Mom was okay with it, I had to let my buried excitement out somewhere. I used a picture of me, Nina, and Scott in our studio and added the caption "So blessed to be asked to make a single with *We the Guilty*. I can't wait!" I added heart emojis for good measure and pressed the button to post. Scott slid onto the bench across from me.

"What kept you?" I asked.

"You know schools. They wanted to know how I was doing after I lost my dad and everything."

I sighed. "How are you doing?"

"I keep thinking he's going to say, 'Hey son, let's go throw the football.'" Scott's voice came out rough as he spoke. "But, I know that's something we'll have to do in Heaven." He reached across the table and squeezed my hand. "It hurts, but I know you know that."

A lump formed in my throat and I nodded. "How's your mom?"

"Well, Dad was our breadwinner," Scott said slowly. "So, Mom has been looking for jobs recently."

I thought about how Mom and Dad used to interview people years ago. I felt awful that Mrs. Carrington would be one of those people at another company because she had to find work at this point in her life—especially after decades of being the sweet homemaker.

"Hey, but what were you doing?" Scott tapped my phone down.

"Posting about our single." I gave him a smile. Posting about the single was a lot safer than YouTube posts about convicting the mayor.

Scott smiled back. "Somehow, that single has been the best thing that's happened to us in a long time."

I let out a tiny laugh at his irony and reached for another fry.

"For real, it's a chance to forget all of it. And it's a chance to praise God and make a difference."

"I know," I sighed. "One single chance at a new life. I'm so excited, I can hardly wait." I reached across the table and hugged him, getting ketchup on my fringe shirt.

"One single chance," Scott echoed. "Any more lyrics?"

I toyed with my French fries and stared at the fluorescent lights before looking back at Scott.

"Scott, I posted that song about justice that I texted you." I lowered my eyes. "And the mayor found the video with my random lyrics about grandpa."

Scott froze and looked at me. "What happened?"

"Mom didn't take it well, and I feel terrible. I thought I was helping. I wanted to make things right once and for all."

Scott reached across the table again and grabbed my hand. "You were and you still are. We have to live like we're striving for eternity or something, even when we can't see the full picture."

I grinned at him. "Or something." We both knew we were chasing Jesus and running our race to meet Him in Heaven. There were no doubts. We just hoped we could make a difference here on earth first, and I prayed God would help me help Mom and that the single would give us our first clue about whether or not He'd use my music talents for ministry.

◆》•◆•《◆

"How's Mom?" I asked when I got home.

Chris met me in the hallway, pulled on his jacket, and gave me a concerned expression. "No food all day. I got some broth in her, but that's about it. I hope she'll eat some toast with you, but she's been queasy. She's keeping the ginger ale companies in business single handedly." Chris reached for the door knob. "She's sleeping now, and I wouldn't wake her. She had three brutal panic attacks back-to-back." Chris' eyes cut me as he stepped out onto the front steps. "I had to take her to urgent care when she told me she was suffocating. We got back about thirty minutes ago. She's finally worn out now with all the medication. Maybe you can stick around tonight and make sure you take care of her."

Tears formed in my eyes as I thought about how rough the day had gone for Mom, while I had enjoyed a day at school with Scott.

"You can't control the panic attacks, Candy. Your mom experienced trauma and is very nervous about what the mayor could truly do to you both." Chris seemed to be reading my mind. "I'd stay, but I did all the online grading I could possibly do. I have to meet with the principal and drumline tonight, so I'll be back tomorrow, okay? Call me if you two need anything." He jogged down the steps into the night.

I shut the door and left the hallway to check on Mom in the living room. She was sleeping soundly again. I knew that would be short lived, so I tiptoed and hoped not to wake her.

Later that night, I sat in bed, looking at the likes my photo got on social. I'd gotten plenty, but as I went back to scroll through the other photos of my friends, I noticed Anna had posted again.

A photo of Anna holding a tiny black and white ultrasound picture greeted me with the caption, "Bumpdate!" The accompanying hashtags **#boymom** and **#teenmom** followed. I didn't know what to say, so I gave it a heart, turned off my phone and tried not to overthink it. I could hear Mom moving around and smiled as soon as she appeared in my bedroom doorframe.

"Sorry I missed dinner with you sweetie." She kissed me on the forehead. "Did you have a good day at school?"

I nodded. I worried about so many things these days–the single with *We the Guilty*, Mom, and Scott, all vied for my heart. I had to do something about it and give it to Jesus. Years ago, homeschooled me wouldn't have known where to turn and I wouldn't have prayed, hoped, or sang for Jesus at all. But, the peace of God reminded me that Jesus ultimately fights and wins our battles. Knowing that calmed my soul. "School was fine," I said.

"That's good news." Mom left after giving me a final peck on the cheek, and I heard her shuffle down the hallway. Somehow, God had used Born Again Records to give me one more shot at having my first single after I'd given it up. I wanted to give it my all now.

"One single chance." I let the words from lunch play over again in my mind. "One single chance."

# Chapter 27: Candy

P RACTICING FOR OUR SINGLE the next night made me forget about my home troubles, even if the studio was at home. Chris had brought the team over from school and we only had an hour to practice before everyone had to be back home. We didn't have long before we had to record the actual single, but we were also posting to YouTube to continue to spread the Good News and promote the band. Tonight, we were filming the video for YouTube, which meant that we practiced the song at least twice before hitting record. Scott and I were in sync, but something was still off.

"Nina, could you give me a longer intro?" I asked, my mic still in my hand. She nodded at me, and complied with her beautiful talent, artistically letting her fingers dance across the piano as she stretched out the intro before I began singing. As I sang, my voice felt different, stronger, and something lit up in me. It wasn't a brief, butterfly spark of joy that usually filled me when I sang. My voice sounded like a wildflower had taken root and started to bloom and my microphone felt like it was made just for me.

❧ ·· • ◆ • ·· ❧

Chris was downstairs helping Mom and Nina had gone to the restroom, so that gave Scott the perfect opportunity to give me a peck on the cheek since we were alone in the studio. "You're threatening me," Scott said in a drawl. "You're threatening to steal my heart, Candy girl. Every time you give me that dimpled smile, my hands are against the wall."

"I don't want to steal your heart, Scott," I let my voice lilt in the most flirtatious way possible. "I want to dance with it."

I lowered my eyes, but Scott slid off his stool, moved closer to me, and lifted my chin with his finger. "I think I'd like that."

Scott took me by the hand and away from the mic. For the second time in our relationship, we danced without music. Maybe we already had each other's hearts or maybe they belonged together.

When I heard Nina's footsteps down the hallway, we let go.

"Forever," Scott whispered, and I turned bright red.

Practice went by quickly as I played and sang next to Scott. Besides being an amazing guitarist, he was the cutest, sweetest, Christian guy in the world. And band or no band, I didn't want to lose him—ever.

# Chapter 28: Leslie

C ANDY HAD MUSICIANS COMING to the house in two weeks. I walked through the kitchen and swiped a finger across the counter. They were professional musicians who would fill the home with technology and equipment to record a single that would be released to the world. And did my house look ready? Of course not. At least not to me. Everything needed to be scrubbed from top to bottom and the living room, well that was a disaster area. I swiped my hair back and wished I'd never fired our housekeeper. I'd been such a different person then. No one wanted to work here now. I couldn't even get a personal assistant. I had to search for a top-notch cleaning service that would do the job. Scrolling through my phone, I came across a few and not knowing which would be the best, scheduled interviews with the top three.

I also needed caterers for the musicians. I took a seat at the table. I needed gluten-free options, dairy free options, allergen free meals and traditional meals that Candy would actually eat. My usual caterers would probably work. I hoped that the musicians would have their own lodging accommodations. I had space for a few people, but not many.

I sank into the kitchen chair and let my face fall into my hands. Candy was really about to sing to the world.

As I spent the day video chatting with my departments and getting updates on the new building, I let myself think about Chris. I enjoyed it when he came over and how sweet he could be, despite my craziness–not that my own craziness had been unwarranted. How many women are in my predicament every day anyway?

The moment Candy came home from school, a pang of mom-guilt hit me as I glanced at my smart watch. I had nothing to make for dinner.

"Love, I'm going to the store." I pecked her on the cheek, and she propped her backpack against the wall.

"Okay," she said. "I sort of told Scott about our history with the mayor. He wants to help out."

This girl.

"We don't need people in our business, Candy. Tell Scott thank you, but not at this time." I reached for a hair tie from the junk drawer. "And go do your homework. Practice the guitar. But please, stay safe. I told you about Jeremy so you could make good judgement calls." I walked towards her and ran a finger down the side of her cheek. "Not dangerous ones."

I knew that the Jeremy Rosewater story would be back in both of our faces, but I refused to tell her that. Instead, I slipped on my heels, grabbed my purse, tossed on my coat, and headed out the door for microwave dinners.

I wondered if Sarah Carrington knew the story about Jeremy, and if she did, who's side was she on?

# Act III: Action

# Chapter 9: Candy

MOM MADE DINNER, AND by "made" I mean she prepared a cold, pop-open salad with cold chicken tossed on top. She didn't even use the microwave ones. The salad had ick written all over it, but I had no other options, so I chewed the rubbery chicken slowly and avoided the tomatoes.

"When you make your single, sweetheart, know that there are going to be a lot of people rooting for you," Mom began slowly. "And because of the family feud, we have a certain number of people who might want to see us hurt."

"Is Mayor Rosewater going to try to stop the single too?" I asked.

"I don't think so," Mom sighed. "But he's not a fan, evident as he's already emailed me and mentioned sound ordinances and potential violations."

"Are you sure you want me to do this?" I asked.

"Yes." Mom aggressively stabbed at her lettuce with her fork. "It's your calling and Mayor Rosewater won't stop either of us."

I noticed Mom looked pale and didn't say too much after dinner. She drank the vanilla flavored drink Chris had brought over the other day, but soon rested on the couch and fell asleep. I worried, though. The Rosewaters kept growing like invasive flowers in our lives. They were like honeysuckle, overtaking, changing, and trying to hurt us.

# Chapter 2: Leslie

"**D**O YOU THINK YOU can have a professional conversation today?" Mayor Rosewater's unkind tone made me flinch.

"I'm ready when you are," I answered and moved forward in my chair. I was grateful we were meeting in my home office today. I felt a little more at ease, even though I knew where this conversation was heading. But I'd mentally prepared for it. Even though we were going to discuss zoning and affordable housing, I would have to reckon with Jeremy Rosewater.

"Let me make this clear." Mayor Rosewater leaned forward in his seat, a sweaty smudge mark on the leather chair I'd offered him. "Seeing you fumble trying to do something with a sinkhole farmland purchase and possibly losing eighty million dollars makes me happy. Watching your building burn on the way home weeks ago also made me kind of happy. Those tubes in your nose kind of make me happy too. I'm not sure how you got them and they do not make me happy enough, but they come close. So, let's talk about the farmland purchase."

*Not happy enough?* I thought.

"Could I get you anything to drink?" I asked, standing to retrieve whatever I could offer.

"No, I'm fine." He unbuttoned his coat. "It shouldn't take too long to talk about zoning, evidence, and Jeremy."

"Jeremy?" My voice came out in a squeak as I sat back down.

"Yes, Jeremy." Mayor Rosewater turned tomato red and leaned forward in his chair. "It's time to even the score, *especially* after you cleared the land I said I wouldn't approve for affordable housing. You're the only woman on earth who would know why I swore on my son's grave to never let a St. John truly succeed—not your parents, not your child, and definitely not you. You'll lose it all, Leslie, all of it, promise." The mayor sneered.

"Mayor, I didn't kill Jeremy," I finally said.

"But you're the reason he died." He hammered each word into my brain and once again, I was a teenager standing in the backyard with a bloodied pink dress. My screams meant nothing.

"My uncle has a weakness," Jeremy had growled at me. "And your dad made him look like a failure. Well, the St. Johns have a weakness too. It's Leslie St. John. Where's your dad to protect you now? No brothers? No fighting skills of your own? You're just a spoiled rich kid. If all your dad has is you, then he is a weak man too."

The words came back to me as Mayor Rosewater sat across the desk. Family member for family member.

*"I hope you never recover."* I heard Jeremy's last words resound in my head like cymbals. I never had. At least not on the inside.

"Am I really the reason?" I twirled in my chair a little and stared at the rain that drizzled down the window next to the bookcase.

"Well, Leslie, if you hadn't been hurt, then Jeremy wouldn't have been killed. So, it really is your fault and we both know that." The mayor clasped his fingers together.

"Oh, and maybe you'd like to tell me about how your daughter made a song about our, uh, family differences."

"Mayor, leave Candy out of this. If you could see past the woman in front of you for an hour and the issue at hand..." My words felt insufficient for the years of hate between our families, but I never wanted it that way. "I was under the impression we were going to discuss affordable housing for our fellow citizens of Honeybrook."

"Leslie." Mayor Rosewater stood and towered over my five-five frame, making me feel at least a foot shorter. "In case you didn't know, Sam died last week."

All the air left my body, and a deflated, but somewhat relieved "I'm so sorry" came out of me. Like I'd thought, Candy would now be safe at her shows and maybe I'd stop freaking out every time we traveled out of state.

"Me too. But funny how when people die, odd things pop up. Like, we both knew my son worked for your dad."

I nodded in agreement.

"I still don't understand what he did or what your dad did, but I do know that Sam had a postcard from Jeremy in his things."

Sweat rolled down the center of my back, each bead clinging to my navy blue blouse.

"A postcard from 1992?" I asked.

The mayor let out a sigh, "Yes, that says, 'Made a mistake at my job. Still glad I went after Leslie, but I expect it will be the end of my time here.'"

*Jeremy wasn't sorry for what he did to me?* I blinked. *What mistake had he made? This had to be after the party when Dad agreed that he wasn't doing a good job. Doing what?*

"The rest of the message has since faded. When Sam got it, he told me I should be worried about Jeremy, but I blew him off, thinking your father was trying to make a man out of him and toughen him up."

For the first time, I saw the mayor sag under the weight of his grief, and my heart ached at the pain my family had caused.

"And for those reasons, I think our zoning conversation should be handled differently. I hope this is our final talk, and you'll understand what I mean by having to pay." Mayor Rosewater cleared his throat and spoke matter-of-factly.

"What do you mean?" I raised my voice. "Sam can't touch Candy at all now. You don't have the power you think you do." I thought about my own postcards.

The mayor narrowed his eyes. "Maybe not. But his dying words were to make sure you were the one that paid and you're right in front of me. Because, after all, you let her post that defamatory video online, and you keep letting her perform. I personally don't think you really care about finding out the truth or helping people that much."

I bit my lip. I cared so much about my daughter, it hurt. And I loved my hometown and everyone who lived here. I knew that video would come back to hurt me. I could still hear the wind blowing furiously, restlessly, as if it too wanted something to be done once and for all.

"Sam never even got this land back," the mayor said. "You and your family are nothing but high-class thieves, and you're hiding evidence."

"This land is the last gift from my parents." My hand trembled as waves of fear beat against my heart. I had just enough evidence to keep me from the police, and I wanted to keep this under the table to protect the family name in case Dad did do something wrong. I wished I hadn't said those things to Jeremy. I wanted to go back in time and tell him "sorry" and that I didn't think he came from losers. He never deserved that from me.

"C'mon, Leslie. This property should have been my brother's. You had to put a request for affordable housing on my desk during an election year, which is why I have to handle you the way I do." Mayor Rosewater leaned forward. "My son started doing work for your father." His voice thundered and each word stung as he said it. "What work it was, I'll never know, but did you ever stop to think about what kind of connections your old man might have to get my son killed in weeks?"

I thought about the postcards from my trunk. I wished for my old teenage journals that had more details than I could remember, but no conclusions. From the postcards alone, mom and dad's notes made even more sense. We were what my mother called "old money," but she also worried about my dad's "past life." I had spent years trying to piece everything together, but failed. Even if Dad had been wrong, he was still my daddy. But what if Jeremy had really done something wrong, and Dad had to protect his team? And even though we both knew my dad most likely had Jeremy killed, there wasn't enough evidence to truly prove it, right? With this new postcard from the mayor, I had enough circumstantial evidence to prove Rosewater retaliated and took the two most important people from my life as a teenager. But I also had evidence to prove my dad could have had Jeremy killed. By who? I didn't know. What did he do? I didn't know that either. It's possible it was all a poorly timed mistake?

The mayor made no mistakes, though. I knew he murdered my parents, but he seemed justified and unapologetic for not just killing my dad, but my innocent mother as well. With tension in the air thick enough to cut, I said, "My dad needed to defend house and home. He took it too far, I agree, but you didn't have to kill both him and my mom in return." I pointed a finger at him.

"You're on family land, Leslie," Mayor Rosewater blustered. "Sam's. And now that he's gone, you will pay."

"My father played fair and square," I sputtered.

"Leslie, your father was a cheat." He moved too close to me, and I leaned my chair against my floor to ceiling bookshelf. "Hypothetically, even if I caused the boating accident–"

Hot, I cut the mayor off. "You caused it," I told him in a low voice.

"You can't prove it." He slammed one hand on the table just as lightning cut the sky, and I jumped. "But you would be the only person who has a shred of evidence if your father wrote anything down or truly sorted the mail when he and Jeremy were 'away.'"

I clenched my fists, trying to stay calm while my family name floated through murky, shameful waters.

"The postcard wasn't among Sam's things marked 'return to sender'. You'd have the return postcard from Sam and anything else your father wrote, saved, or documented suggesting I wanted to get even, which I'm not saying I did. If I run for office and you are denied zoning for what the idiotic public thinks is a good idea, then I'd have to get rid of the one person in my way. Getting rid of one takes care of hundreds of other problems, don't you see?"

"What makes you think I have evidence?" I challenged. "I was a teenager when my parents were killed."

"If I don't have the return postcard and it wasn't in Jeremy's or Sam's things, you have to have it. It's why I have to stop you."

*Would he know about the note too?* I thought. Would he have a clue about the note that Dad had written me years ago–the only piece of paper that suggested that he worried that the mayor would take revenge on him.

"Why evidence about our families now?" I asked, stalling for time, knowing I'd never admit I had a note from Dad written right before his death–or the return postcard from Sam Rosewater from thirty years ago–until my case was bulletproof.

"Rob's not here to protect you, Leslie!" Mayor Rosewater practically roared. "This morning, I found the proof I needed about my son–the postcard Sam only told me about–so stop playing hard and difficult games with me. We will end this this week."

I shook from the pressure. *Sure, I had some evidence. But, even if I did, it wouldn't bring my parents back. Did I want justice for them? Sure. But then, my dad had Jeremy killed, so...* I blinked myself to the present as thunder echoed in the distance.

"Stop it," I shouted. "It is the right of every American citizen to have the opportunity to work to try to put a roof over their heads at night." I kept my voice raised and leaned forward on my desk. "As a business owner, I want to extend that to all people who are working day and night, trying to do their best, because some of us are living very well and doing their dirtiest work."

"Are you suggesting me?" The mayor raised an eyebrow at me.

I took a sip of coffee and returned the glare. I wouldn't let him get to me. I couldn't.

My heartbeat drowned out the sound of him standing up. He stepped behind the chair and put his hands on the back of it.

"Something has to give, Leslie. At least the evidence about your dear old father is mine," Mayor Rosewater said. "Maybe you could get the zoning deal in exchange for the evidence. How about that?"

"How do you know I have anything?" I tried to maintain a steady voice.

"Sam always wrote back to Jeremy. And coming across this postcard this morning proves your family—" The mayor cut off and blinked back emotion. "I know your dad wrote down everything too. Not to mention what Candy alluded to as well." I shifted in my chair. "If I give you hypothetical evidence, what happens next?" I chewed my lip. It would be much simpler just to give the evidence, but if my dad had done dirty work instead of being a spy, I felt I owed it to my family to keep it. My heart wanted safety for me and Candy and affordable housing for Honeybrook. Did God understand that?

"All property is mine," I stated.

"Well, there you have it."

The mayor and I said uneasy goodbyes, and I decided now was as good a time as any to go online and buy my first Bible. I believed that every question I ever had could be answered if I read it.

# Chapter 3: Leslie

T HE NEXT NIGHT, I sat down at the kitchen table with my microwaved dinner and reached for my phone to check the time. Candy had been out with Scott for quite a while. I reached down and slid off my heels and smiled to myself. Those kids were getting quite serious. As I straightened, my eyes traveled to the door cracked open that led to our beach backyard. Were they outside?

I stood to check, but the lights were off. I opened the door a little more.

"Candy?" I called. The waves crashed against the shore in response.

Not seeing them, I turned back inside and my heart froze in place as I locked eyes with Mayor Rosewater, rustling through the living room table drawer.

"This never happened, if you know what's good for you," Mayor Rosewater said and wagged a finger at me. "You had a chance to give me the postcard and you didn't." His voice cracked as he spoke.

*He's going to kill me. I'm alone and he's about to make this all look like a mistake,* I thought. *He was serious yesterday. Was it all about to stop here?*

I sank to the floor, desperate. "Please, don't do this."

"There's no one to run interference for you, Leslie, no one. And now I know that you have to have the return postcard. My brother always wanted justice for Jeremy, as do I."

I shook in my spot, wishing Chris would at least call.

Mayor Rosewater yanked me up by my hair. "You have my postcard–the one I wrote and the one with the most evidence about your dad and my son. I know you have it," he whispered through gritted teeth, "so show me your part of the evidence and we'll put everything together now."

"Mayor, please, let me go!" I tried to struggle free as he dragged me up the steps. My heart thudded in my chest, and I kept pressing against his aggressive shoving all the way to the top floor. A fresh round of fear filled me, but so did anger. *How dare he?* He pulled me to the room with the chest, as if he'd scouted out the house before I'd arrived.

"I've waited thirty years to make you lose all that mattered." He held me against the wall with one, hairy arm. "But now?"

"Mayor," I choked out the words. "Whatever my dad did– good or bad– I'm sorry it resulted in Jeremy's death."

"Me too." Mayor Rosewater scanned the room. "And what good could your father have done to have everything about my son written off as an accident?'"

"I don't know," I gasped. It was a matter of time before anxiety set in. I tried not to look at the chest. The mayor couldn't take those items before I could connect the dots.

"I thought Jeremy's wallet was destroyed in the crash." He shoved me towards the chest. "I found it in Sam's things."

"Mayor–" I couldn't force myself to give up my family's history and my lungs couldn't handle anymore either. "I can't breathe."

"I thought your dad got rid of that postcard I wrote him too."

The incriminating postcard flashed before my eyes about his haunting my family. He wanted it, truly feared I'd expose it, and was about to end our feud tonight. But I never planned on him ending it this way when I didn't have a leg to stand on.

"Mayor!" I begged one last time, but he raised a hand to my face and my skin stung before everything went black.

# Chapter 4: Candy

SOMETHING DIDN'T FEEL RIGHT when I got home and it wasn't because Scott didn't walk with me. I pushed open the door, walked to the kitchen, and saw Mom's unfinished dinner on the table. She always threw her trash out. I heard rustling upstairs and raced up the steps. The light in the spare room was on, and I practically slid in my socks down the hallway to see why.

"Mom?" I looked around, but heard nothing. My stomach lurched when I glanced down at my feet. She was on the floor and looked gray.

"Mom?" I shouted. "Mom!"

She didn't answer. I looked around the room and noticed nothing out of the ordinary. I knelt down next to her.

"What happened?" I shook her shoulders, and she winced.

"Candy," Mom whispered and from the glaze in her eyes, I'd missed something awful. Her hair stuck out in all directions, and she still wouldn't move.

"I'm going to get help, Mom." I tried to stay calm, even though a tornado was brewing inside me. Someone or something had to initiate a panic attack. Who or what would cause this and leave Mom on the floor? I ran downstairs to find my cell phone, only to see a large, shadowy figure hunched over and creeping through the side door.

It was definitely a who, not a what. Too scared to speak, I let whoever it was go. As soon as the door slammed behind him or her, I activated our smart house.

"Kelly, call 911." I hoped the panic in my voice wouldn't mess up voice recognition. "What's your emergency?" The landline phone immediately switched to our overhead speaker.

"My mom is unconscious." I backed up against the wall scanning the kitchen for a sidekick, evil henchman, or any other nightmarish person I'd read about in American Literature. "She has COPD and really bad anxiety. It looks like someone attacked her."

"Do you have any idea who? An ex-boyfriend?" the operator prompted.

My throat almost closed. "No, not an ex, but I don't know who for sure." I rubbed my clammy hands against my jeans.

"Police and ambulance are on their way."

I ran back upstairs to check on Mom.

She was awake, but gasping for air.

"Mom, help is coming," I told her.

Mom started shaking uncontrollably. "I wanted to believe your grandfather could have been a spy. Or that maybe Jeremy crossed sides and fought for the enemy." Her lips started turning blue, and she couldn't stand.

"What happened?" I asked.

Mom squeezed my arm. "We were yelling."

I almost rolled my eyes. Mom mid-panic attack never gave good answers. A huge thud froze both of us. It sounded like the army was coming up the steps.

"Police, freeze!"

I exhaled. I'd never been more grateful to see so many officers together in my life.

"Put your hands on your head where we can see them."

I obeyed, but Mom's traumatized expression indicated she needed the stretcher. In the heat of the moment, she blacked out again, but this time she didn't wake up.

◆》 ·· ◆ ·· 《◆

"How's Mom?" I asked hours after waiting in the emergency room. I'd texted Chris on the way over as well as Scott.

Chris sat across from me, looking pensive.

He didn't answer right away, as if he were searching for the words. "Mom is fragile," he began slowly, "and tonight not only hurt her, but it set her back."

"Chris Schaffer?" A nurse came out in pink scrubs. "Leslie is asking for you as well as her daughter."

I bounced up, more terrified than relieved. Allegedly Mom wasn't responding well, and they only let one visitor in at a time, starting with Chris. Oddly enough, the more I heard coming from her room, the more scared I became and grateful to be second.

"It's okay, Leslie," Chris said. "I'm here."

I heard Mom's panicked voice followed by nurses. "Lots of people wet the bed here and they throw up too, honey." The voice of an old woman came from Mom's room. "There's nothing to be ashamed of."

The silver-haired woman walked outside and stared at me for a full minute. "Your mom will be ready to talk to you in a moment, darlin'."

I nodded and glanced at Chris as soon as he stepped out. "What happened?"

Chris' eyes clouded over. "Trauma. Mom can't make sense of tonight, but she's blaming herself for everything."

"We're not talking about any problems." A tall doctor stood over both of us. "We have to keep Mom calm."

"Chris!" Mom screamed and Chris rushed back, leaving me alone in the hallway.

I tried to ignore the stench coming from Mom's room mixed with the smell of everyone else's dinners. Fidgeting with my shirt and glancing around, I tried to focus on what would happen to Mom next. I blinked and looked up to see Scott's familiar frame coming towards me.

"Hey Candy." Scott's face twisted in concern, and I immediately fell into his arms. He returned the hug tightly. "What happened?"

"Someone broke in. I think it was the mayor," I said.

"What?" Scott immediately let go, and stared me in the eyes, showing his confusion.

"Miss, you can't share details about the incident with anyone until after the investigation is complete." I didn't notice the short police officer standing near the counter a little further down the hallway. He walked over to us with a thick pad in his hand and a blue pen. "Who are you?" He directed his question to Scott.

"Scott Carrington."

"What do you know about the Chancellors and the Rosewaters?"

"My girlfriend told me that the two families were having trouble, that's all." Scott stayed vague, which I appreciated.

I heard Mom retching from her room and nurses kept coming back and forth with water and blankets. Chris walked out of the room this time, too, wearing a worried expression.

"Okay," the officer said. "But you two need to talk about something else tonight, okay?"

"Yes, sir," I nodded.

216

The officer left and Scott squeezed my hand. Inside the room, Mom shrieked, and instant tears poured down my face. Chris went back to her room, but Scott pulled me closer as we stood in the hallway.

"How can I help?" he asked.

"Thanks for showing up," I said. "Just standing here while we wait means more than you think."

Scott hugged me a little longer, but when the nurse told us Mom could have visitors, he gave me the 'I'll-call-you' sign with his hand and left. We tried to keep Mom calm once we walked in, but she kept circling back in her mind to Jeremy, the boating accident, and the mayor. Her fears about how else he might plan to hurt us seemed to grow by the second.

Chris sat on the edge of the hospital bed in the darkened room and I sat in between them.

"Is Mom going to get better?" I asked.

Mom's crestfallen expression sparked fear, but Chris rubbed Mom on the back softly. "In a few days, we'll be able to take Mom home again, and she should be a lot better."

"Days?" I asked.

Chris only nodded this time.

A police officer knocked at Mom's door, then walked in, closing it softly behind him.

"Hello, ma'am. I'm just here to write down what you remember happening about tonight, okay? Take your time."

Mom immediately began to shake and Chris intervened. "I'm not sure Leslie is ready, officer."

"This should only take a moment," the officer pressed.

"We were mad." Mom didn't say who it was. "He yelled at me and spilled coffee on me."

I blinked in shock. There hadn't been coffee anywhere. The tiny pulse oximeter on Mom's finger wiggled as she pointed to her face. "He hit me hard."

"Who?" the officer asked.

Mom looked at me. "I don't know."

Chris sank down into the chair across from Mom, and my eyes grew wet from frustration.

"Ma'am, there's no sign of a break-in at your house, and there were no coffee stains on your clothing. You have no bruises." The police officer delivered the words softly. "Are you sure you're talking about tonight?" He placed his notepad down and sat in the swivel chair next to Mom's bed.

Mom nodded, and I held her hand.

"I saw someone who kind of looked like Mayor Rosewater," I said.

The police officer raised an eyebrow. "That's a heavy statement, young lady. Your mom has no evidence and you're going to suggest a long-standing government official broke into your house?"

Okay, so it sounded much worse when it blurted out of my mouth than when I thought about it. But the figure favored the hateful old man and who else would want to hurt Mom and me? Wouldn't the officer at least write it down? I mean, didn't my word count for something? The angry tornado inside me spun faster.

"I'll take it down," the officer said, his eyes turning soft. "But we've been to your house and we don't see signs of anything being out of place."

Mom said nothing, but I felt her growing cold.

Chris seemed to believe me.

Mom looked confused. "Did I do something wrong?"

The police officer stood up to leave, and Mom's doctor returned.

"A man hurt me," Mom said earnestly. "And he spilled my coffee."

"Leslie's one of our former trauma patients. She's having trouble remembering what exactly happened." The doctor spoke in low tones to me, Chris and the officer. "Whatever truly happened, she mentally blocked it and saved the fewest memories possible," the doctor whispered. "We think she's had a bad panic attack again, that's all. Nothing she said makes sense or adds up." The doctor kept his voice low and out of Mom's earshot. "Leslie's a sweetheart, though. We'll keep an eye on her."

Mom gripped her stomach in pain and glanced at me and Chris. Did Mom forget or was she trying to protect us? Or even more like her, was she trying to help the people of Honeybrook once and for all?

***

Since I suggested to the police the mayor had broken in, they detained him for questioning. The officers came back the next day and informed us that the mayor said mom expected him, forgot, and he only opened the door that evening, but not for criminal purposes. Who would have thought the door was unlocked and he never had to break anything? Being the mayor, with no previous history, and since Mom couldn't make heads or tails of a new puppy if she tried, the mayor remained free for the moment–but an investigation had been launched. Meanwhile, Mom stayed in the hospital for two more days, as doctors were concerned about her psychological welfare. By Monday evening, several discharge papers were signed and Chris and I took her home.

"Candy, did you see Mayor Rosewater?" Mom whispered that night at the kitchen table. "It was definitely a man." She ran her fingers down my hair. "But I don't want to make things worse with him if we don't have to."

"I mean, it looked like him." I stabbed a piece of broccoli and glanced at Chris. "It really did."

"The police are going to investigate your house again, the mayor's house, the mayor's office, and anywhere else that could be of interest," Chris said. "Your house didn't show much, but it's pretty big."

Mom blinked at both of us and my heart sank as she stuttered, scrambling for words and memories. "But everything went wrong here," Mom said.

"There's no proof." Chris squeezed Mom's hand. "Not unless you can think of anything else," he added. "They couldn't find anything at the mayor's house."

"What did he steal?" Mom shot both of us a questioning expression.

"It might come back to you," Chris sighed. "If it was Rosewater, he made a neat escape with whatever he took."

Mom closed her eyes, and Chris helped her to the couch. There was nothing we could do for now, anyway. Mom wanted to make the world a better place and the mayor wanted to destroy ours. What would God want us to do?

# Chapter 5: Candy

THE BEAUTY OF BEING a singer is having a home away from home. Sure, our studio was at the house, but I didn't have to think about mayor troubles for a while. We had days before *both* our debut single and our feature with *We the Guilty* were to be recorded, and I wouldn't have been more excited if it were my birthday. I was spreading the Gospel, making music, making a difference, and making so many precious, beautiful, moments I used to only dream of. And, performing with Scott only made life better. Scott's smile alone made me think 'Mayor who-water?' I skipped into the house and saw Mom and Chris in the kitchen. Chris had a colander full of lettuce, and Mom sat at the table, sipping the doctor-suggested nutritional drink before dinner.

"How was school, honey?" Mom asked.

I slid my backpack down onto the kitchen floor. "Great! I got an A on my English paper," I said.

"Congratulations." Chris smiled at me.

"Wonderful job, sweetie." Mom stood to hug me.

"Are you okay?" I asked.

"You know that old second dose." Mom tried to laugh and wobbled the pill bottle from the counter in her hand, but I glanced at Chris.

"Maybe you can convince your mom to take it." Chris' cheerful expression over my grades switched to frustration.

"Chris, I told you what I wanted." Mom sounded equally irritated.

"Leslie, this is normal, but I'm not letting you go back there."

I slowly sat down across from Mom. "What do you want, Mom?"

"A smoke and a shot of brandy," Mom sighed. "Not a second dose that will make me sick."

I froze. Did this drama with the mayor push her back to her old habits?

"Mom, you can't do that," I said.

"I don't want a second dose of meds that sometimes makes me sick." Mom glared at Chris. "I don't understand what's wrong with a cheat day."

"Leslie, you're almost one hundred days clean." Chris tried to convince her, but she restlessly tapped the table, then stood. She reached into her purse and pulled out a lighter, then stepped out the back door. I didn't know whether or not she had cigarettes hidden behind the house, but my heart started to race.

"Give her some space. This is all part of her healing." Chris patted me on the back. "Mom has to work through this on her own."

Tears clouded my view of our beach, but I saw Mom standing at the edge of the water, the wind whipping her hair.

"What did you want for dinner?" Chris asked, trying to distract me from the view outside.

"Whatever is fine."

Mom was kneeling on the ground now, and I wasn't sure if she was crying, praying, or both.

"Let Mom work it out," Chris said and gave me a soft nudge away from the window. He started working on dinner, and we moved around the kitchen in complete silence. My brain almost exploded with worry for Mom, and I chewed my fingernails, hoping she'd do the right thing.

"Reckoning with a nightmare is painful, and your mom is just uncovering hers." Chris shattered the tension as we waited. "Unfortunately, she doesn't have–" we were interrupted by Mom re-entering, sand blowing across the kitchen floor and her frantically gasping for air.

"The wind took your breath away?" Chris calmly moved over to Mom. "Let's sit down and find your inhaler."

Mom started coughing, and I wanted to run away. If she went back to smoking, she'd only get worse. Didn't she care about us at all?

"Just the inhaler," Chris said. "We're not doing a second dose."

Mom nodded and took the inhaler.

"What happened to the lighter?" I asked nervously.

Mom let out a soft sigh. "I tossed it in the water." She crossed her legs and set the inhaler on the table. "It needs to be in the past and it's dangerous." She pointed to her oxygen tank.

My heart warmed. *Mom wouldn't smoke again?*

"Candy, why don't you play something on the guitar before dinner, like we did years ago?" Mom asked.

Shocked by the unusual request, I ran upstairs to grab my guitar, but my gaze fell on Daddy's old acoustic guitar next to it. It suddenly felt so wrong for me to leave the familiar old instrument in its case next to my bed. I slid it out and ran my hand over the honey-colored guitar with its dark chocolate neck. Dinner and guitar had been our thing and it pinched at my heart. I squeezed both guitars in each of my hands, letting the cool, steel strings calm my nerves. I held Daddy's guitar a little closer as I left my room with both.

I couldn't look Chris in the eyes when I came down-stairs and gave the acoustic guitar to him. "It's a duet," I said. "Daddy and I played duets at dinner."

Chris seemed caught off guard, but then took the guitar from me. "Let's do it."

We sat around the kitchen table, forming the tiniest semi-circle, and I sang my half of the song that would go forever unanswered.

"I'm growin' up tomorrow..." I sang as my heart slowly melted like butter, each word exiting without Daddy gaz-ing back at me.

A few tears slid down my cheeks, but Chris kept pace with me and encouraged me with his eyes the whole way through.

"Won't you show me how?" I ended the song and Mom started crying and hugging me at the same time. I start-ed crying too. Chris placed Daddy's guitar next to his chair and bear-hugged us at the same time. We weren't the backyard-guitar-on-the-beach family anymore. Mom could barely handle the cold, windy weather, and I'd grown up way more than I ever thought I'd have to. We were a completely new version of how I envisioned being seventeen. The only constants in my life were Jesus and country music, and I was holding on to those tighter than a rodeo cowboy. Only, I didn't have the luxury of holding on for eight seconds, then falling off like the cowboys did. I had to hold on to keep my family together. Chris and I played more songs until it grew late, and Mom clapped for us, looking happier than she had earlier that afternoon. Her high, tinkly laugh returned, and Chris pecked her on the cheek before leaving. I zipped up my guitar case and gave Mom a hug before turning in myself. More important than music, I had to spend time talking to Jesus about Mom, the mayor, and then maybe my music.

# Chapter 6: Candy

I SPUN IN FRONT of my mirror getting ready to perform for our next YouTube song. Our views had increased some, and I thought we'd gotten the bump because we'd started to sing more upbeat tunes. I hoped Scott would like my dress. At school, he'd given me a tilted smile with a wink when I wore my patchwork jeans, and well, I practically died and came back as a princess. I had to up my game for our next video tonight. The soft, dusty pink dress came with a swing skirt. I thought about putting a fringe white vest over it, but decided against it, thinking it would be too much. I slid on my white cowgirl boots and fluffed my hair a little. I knew the songs were for Jesus, but somewhere inside, I wanted Scott to think I looked cute tonight too.

I jogged downstairs to wait for the crew to arrive. Chris was bringing them, but they were running late since it was past four-thirty.

Mom came over to the stairs where I sat waiting. "Why are you wearing that?" Her voice came out in a panicked screech.

"It's for the video." Her screeching worried me. "We're not just practicing today."

Mom became hard. "I don't even remember you having that dress. When did you get it?" She sat down next to me and alarm bells went off in my head. *What was wrong?*

"I ordered it last month with my allowance," I answered, smoothing it out and trying to stay cool.

"The cut of that dress makes it look too short. Change it. It's not the dress for tonight."

And not let Scott see this dress? So much for staying calm. "But, Mom!" I argued. "It's brand new!"

The doorbell rang and I heatedly raced to open the door. Chris stood there with his shoulder bag and froze. "You look just like your mother in that dress." His voice came out rough, and he hesitated before speaking again. "The spring dance in our senior year of high school..." Chris walked in slowly and looked at Mom. "Leslie, Candy is the spitting image of–"

Mom raised a hand. "I know and she's going to change. I didn't know she had a dress like that."

Chris nodded.

"Why do I have to change?" I demanded, crossing my arms defiantly.

"I said so." Mom frowned at me before standing. "I didn't say you could buy a dress and–"

"It's literally two inches longer than my other cream one I wore to the county fair," I interrupted.

Mom's eyes widened, and she arched her eyebrows at me. "I told you that's not the appropriate dress for a YouTube video."

"I'm not taking it off," I rebutted. "You're not being fair."

"Or you won't make the video," Mom challenged. "The decision is yours."

My heart began to race like horses right out of the gate.

Mom bit her lip. "Chris, can you tell the kids they can't make the video tonight?"

Heat filled me. She just told me I could make the decision. I leaned over the banister. "Since we're not making the video, I'm wearing this to dinner," I stated.

Mom squinted her eyes at me. "Don't use that tone with me, Candace." I stomped up the steps, but not before I heard Mom telling Chris, "It looks just like the dress I was wearing the night Jeremy attacked me."

"I remember you wearing that dress for the other dance in the spring too," Chris agreed.

"I can't see it right now, not with everything that's going on with Rosewater," Mom whispered.

She wanted to make me change because of Jeremy?! I ran to my bedroom and slammed the door. No video, no Scott, no anything? Her anxiety ruined even my wardrobe?! I burst into tears on my bed and hugged my pillows close to my chest. Why was life so hard? I sobbed for what felt like an eternity, and I glanced over at my mirror–my red, puffy eyes and runny nose looking back at me. My pink dress, wrinkled and creased now, seemed less dreamy. How was I supposed to know Mom wore a pink dress like this on the night Jeremy attacked her?

I heard Mom downstairs and the clinking sound of glasses. I hadn't heard that sound in months, and my heart stopped.

"Are you ready to talk?" Chris asked from outside the door.

"Why are you still here?" I asked.

"Candy, I expect more from you," Chris said.

I got up and opened the door. I stepped into the hallway and didn't say anything.

"Your Mom didn't deserve that," Chris said. "We're helping her stay clean and avoiding her top ten painful triggers is a good way to do that."

"Why do I have to obey if she's the one that needs psychiatric help?" I crossed my arms. "She's always going to be sick."

"Candy!" Chris seemed surprised. "That's disrespectful. I left your mother downstairs, and she is not in a good space at all. When you gave up the single, that was out of love. Loving one another, inside and outside of romance, means showing up for the little things too. Love doesn't have to be as big as giving up a single. It can look like respecting someone's feelings. Or, you could have taken this moment to show other fruits of the Spirit, like kindness, goodness, or self-control."

A wave of conviction came over me, and the dress suddenly didn't mean all that much.

"How's Mom?" I asked.

"Disappointed in you," Chris said.

"Can I apologize?"

"Not at this moment." Chris leaned against the door. "Give her a chance to cool off."

"I didn't want to hurt her." I started crying again.

"I know." Chris moved to hug me.

I wanted to make it right and show true love. Mayor Rosewater and Jeremy were stressing out Mom. Me reminding her of how it started and what she wore didn't help. So now I had to fix it and it would start with me changing my dress.

# Chapter 7: Leslie

I WANTED TO MANAGE my anxiety better. I buttoned up my shirt in the bathroom mirror, then ran a comb through my hair. Twice a week therapy, Alcoholics Anonymous, and I'd still been triggered by the dress that started everything. I didn't want to be that "Nervous Nancy" for life. I took a deep breath, as practiced, and let it out slowly. Today was a new day and a chance to stay calm.

I walked down the stairs, adjusting my collar, only to meet Candy in the kitchen.

"Can we talk?" Candy asked.

"Of course." I sorted through the fruit in the basket on the table.

"I wanted to say I'm sorry for being inconsiderate of your feelings last night." Candy's eyes clouded over. "I didn't know how much the dress meant to you..."

"You were pretty disrespectful last night." I peeled a banana slowly. "But I forgive you." I gazed outside for a moment. "I'm working on it," I told her. "I'm working on the anxiety while being clean, but it's not easy."

Candy's face softened and she came over to hug me. I squeezed her back. I promised myself I wouldn't freak out over any more dresses and smiled as Candy practically skipped out the door for school.

I sat down in my home office and clicked through my emails. Rosewater's office, not the mayor himself, sent me an email about a potential lawsuit? Allegations of defamation of character? I narrowed my eyes at the email. "Oliver Rosewater is not the kind of person who would attack his constituents in any way, shape, or form." I let out a laugh and pressed one hand to my head. I thought he broke in? What was he trying to do now?

My phone rang.

"Leslie Chancellor."

"Leslie." I heard the mayor's rough voice and my heart stopped. "I know that decision making is hard for you, but you're running out of time."

"What kind of decision, Mayor?" I asked, my heart racing.

"Tell the officers nothing," he snapped, and I was cut off by a distinct click.

I wracked my brain for the memories of the break in a few days ago. Candy was right. It had been him. I saw him now, standing in the kitchen with his signature black coat. I saw Candy and the postcards, and I could hear shouting. There was so much shouting... but nothing else. Had he knocked, and Candy didn't know about his coming? Had I agreed to let him take the postcards in some sort of compromise? Did I black out, and he'd been fed up with me and just left? It didn't feel right. But I couldn't remember, even if someone shook me upside down. I dared not say anything at all. Even if one postcard incriminated the mayor, the other two pointed a finger at my dad, and I refused to let that into the open.

I took off my readers and stood to walk through the kitchen, mechanically solving the problem. I took out four coffee mugs and lined them up along the counter. Then I went upstairs to my room. In my mini fridge, behind all the apple cider, sparkling water, and iced coffee, sat a masquerading bottle of vintage wine. Candy had missed it. Chris never guessed I had it, but I had always known about it. And today, with the mayor attacking me, my building destroyed, and not knowing what to really tell God, I popped open the bottle and went downstairs to fill the coffee mugs. I'd had enough.

Chris was supposed to come over for lunch, but I had time to unwind before he'd ever notice. With three mugs in hand, I stepped outside and began to slowly let the calming effects of my favorite red wine relax my nerves. The wind blew my hair, and I remembered enjoying drinks with Rob on the same beach. The sand danced over my toes, and the saltwater air brought back memories of when Candy was little and we were teaching her to play the guitar. I reached for my second mug and started drinking. I heard the phone ringing–probably Chris. I loved him, and I wanted him here, but he couldn't see me now. As I let the first empty mug roll into the sand, guilt consumed me. I hadn't made it to one hundred days clean. I failed. And for those reasons, I decided it wasn't worth it to stop now.

❧ ·•◆•· ❦

"Leslie?" I heard Chris' voice and I cracked open my eyes, surprised.

"Why are we on the floor?" I mumbled, and swiped at the weird grittiness on my lip.

"We're on the sand in the backyard," Chris said. "Why do you smell like a bar?"

"Chris, Mayor Rosewater might–" I stopped and started crying.

"Les', I don't care right now if Rosewater is going to the moon." Chris reached down and grabbed my arm. "Can't you tell you're drunk?" He crossed his arms in annoyance.

"What?" Everything had blurry edges now, and if shame were a jacket, I would be wearing it. I tried to stand up, but stumbled close to the sliding glass doors. "I'm not drunk," I said. "I only had three."

Chris followed me and slipped one hand around my waist as we stepped into the kitchen. I reached for the last coffee mug, but tripped and fell on the cold tile floor. I started laughing. "I guess I missed that last shot."

"Leslie, listen to me." Chris knelt next to me, sweating and his hand felt clammy as he grabbed mine. "I'm taking you to the hospital. You're turning blue."

"I'm not blue," I snapped. "Wouldn't I know if I was blue? I'm happier now than I've been in a long time."

"Les', that's not what I mean." Chris's words didn't make sense, but somehow I ended up in his car. I wasn't able to finish the last drink.

"Candy's coming home soon," I mumbled.

"We'll call her," Chris said.

"She can't see me like this," I said.

"She'll understand."

I didn't think she would, but suddenly I couldn't think at all. My throat started closing. The car closed in around me, and I couldn't breathe. "Help me," I choked.

Chris turned gray and pulled over, immediately dialing 911 as my stomach threatened to empty its contents all over the car. I pushed open the car door just in case and Chris patted me on the back.

"I failed." I started crying again as I fell back into the seat. "God is so upset with me." I gulped for bits of air. "And Candy will be too." I blinked back tears as my eyeliner stung my eyes. "It's all ruined!" I wasn't even a Christian, and I didn't really deserve any more chances. The dashboard in front of me blurred and I struggled to breathe. I kept gasping for air and everything started to spin. I heard Chris praying out loud, and I wished for faith like that. All I had was the tiniest hope in the world that maybe God would let me live long enough to tell Him I was sorry.

&lt;•»—•◆•—«•&gt;

"Mom started drinking again?" I heard Candy's voice.

"Mom had a slip up." I heard Chris' response, and I blinked myself awake.

"What time is it?" I asked.

"You stayed overnight. It's nine o'clock in the morning," Chris said. "Wednesday."

I tried to sit up and look at both of them. "Guys, I'm really sorry," I said in a low voice. "I thought I could handle a one-day binge."

"You stopped breathing in the car." Chris' tone wobbled a little. "The ambulance met us on the road."

"I'm so sorry," I whispered. "I don't know how I can make it up to the both of you."

"Just stop," Candy said with enough saltiness in her tone that showed her hurt.

I'd failed. My heart whispered a plea of forgiveness to God, hoping He'd understand.

"Easy." Chris took Candy's hand. "We get to start at day one again."

I couldn't stop crying, and Chris came over to hug me. "What's scaring you?" I appreciated the whispered tone.

"The mayor is going to destroy me," I whispered back. "And he might win."

# Chapter 8: Candy

"**T**HANK YOU GUYS FOR what you did," Mom said softly once we were home and the three of us were in the living room. "I think some wounds are too deep to heal, though. I'm going to have to handle the mayor head on."

In that moment, Mom looked much older than Chris, even though he had sprouted a few strands of gray hair in the last few months.

"Candy," Mom said, pulling me close while looking at Chris. "You need to know more about the mayor story I told you in case one day I'm not here." Mom looked down and smoothed out her shirt.

"Mom," I said and moved closer to her. "Isn't it just because of the thing with Jeremy?"

"Mostly." She bit her lip.

"You're not giving up, are you?" I asked.

"Honey..." Mom grasped my hands into hers and her eyes clouded over. "Jeremy had no right to beat me senseless. However drunk he may have been, he knew my parents had become a lot richer because of your grandfather and Sam Rosewater's gambling problems. When Mayor Oliver Rosewater neatly staged the boating accident, I always knew it would be me next. The Rosewaters have always had a 'scorch earth' attitude about things. How I know that is another story, but this is land your grandfather gave me as a high school graduation present. He told me everything was good." Mom choked out the words. She flushed red. "I'm standing my ground on this, okay? If the mayor wants it back, he'll have to go to war with me first. But if I lose, you know the story."

I blinked–half-excited, half-nervous.

"You think I've lost it." Mom laughed at me and repositioned on the couch. "Honey, I've been in business for a long time. There are nonviolent ways of winning a war, you know."

"Or we can listen to what the police say." Chris grabbed the remote. "And not stress out and maybe stay out of the hospital for a few weeks."

Mom rolled her eyes. "Seriously, Chris?"

As they teased, a tiny little seed fell into my heart. *Consider how the wild flowers grow. They do not labor or spin. Yet I tell you, not even Solomon in all his splendor was dressed like one of these.* The verse Chris had shared with us at youth group popped into my head. The part about how Jesus said not to worry about tomorrow because God took care of His people. Would God use me to take care of this land problem with Mom?

"Can you get the mail, honey?" Mom asked me. "I need to see if we've been sent any other updates."

Chris gave me a warm smile as I stood to leave, stepping into the muggy March afternoon.

At the base of the mailbox were a sprinkle of uncut wildflowers, and I paused to admire them. I knew wildflowers grew in the winter in our corner of the south, but it was already early March. They were so beautiful. I opened the mailbox and grabbed the pile of mail before I reached down to pluck a bright pink flower and a tender lavender one to study them with my free hand. Carefree wildflowers. I saw a letter about my personal property on the outskirts of Honeybrook–the waterfront property one. I twisted the flowers in my fingers, wishing my life were as carefree as them. I had a mom inside I might lose because she refused to cower to the mayor of Honeybrook. She planned to fight for Daddy's dream, and she wasn't going to leave the land my grandpa left her–bad blood or not. I thought about my single and how mom agreed to meet *We the Guilty* halfway so I could still chase my dreams.

Willoughby waved to me from next door, and I politely waved back. He rolled up the trashcans for Ms. Rosewater and I saw her mail tucked under his arm.

The wind picked up and I thought about Daddy. He'd pray and he'd help Mom. I had tried to handle things myself with the song, but that had flopped. Was I even helping at all? I thought about the whole situation. Is this my second chance? Could I ease Mom's anxiety and show love or kindness instead of judging her about it? I thought about my land that had been gifted to me at Christmas. I thought I'd build a studio on it or maybe my first house. But now, seeing Mom fight for the affordable housing project, maybe my land needed to bring peace and healing once and for all. Maybe like the verse, I just needed to let all my worries go and let Jesus handle it.

Per youth group Fruit of the Spirit challenge, we were supposed to bear fruit and Jesus would take care of the rest, just like He took care of the wildflowers.

When I came inside and took off my coat, Chris shushed me as I tromped through the kitchen. Mom was sleeping on the couch. "Is Mom okay?" I asked.

Chris' eyes softened. "Your mom is just really tired. It's been a long day."

She slept so hard we had to wake her up for the dinner Chris made.

"What time is it?" Mom croaked.

"Almost seven." Chris sat a plate of food down in front of her. I sat down on the couch beside her. Mom reached for a fork and took a bite of ravioli. "This is good, thank you." She chewed slowly.

Chris smiled and sat down across from us. Mom ate, but didn't say much. She looked as if she were going to cry the entire time but didn't. Instead, she nibbled through half of the meal and then started to fall asleep again.

"Les', let's get you off the couch and ready for bed," Chris said.

Mom numbly nodded and gave me a peck on the head. "Night, sweetie." She stood and yawned. "I guess we can turn in." I heard her soft footsteps pad up the stairs.

I headed to the kitchen for a glass of water and noted Chris stayed at the base of the steps, ensuring Mom made it upstairs.

That night, after he left, I checked on Mom too. She slept heavily, as if trying to catch up on years of missed sleep. I left her alone. Plus, I had late-night plans to work on.

I needed to figure out how to turn my land into an affordable housing project. Despite not wanting to be a part of the family business, I'd have to make the sacrifice. It wouldn't be my first project, after all. After faith came family, and like a wildflower, I knew I was changing. It was weird, especially since I knew I wouldn't have turned over property years ago when Daddy was alive. I also wouldn't have cared what happened to the company. Only my dreams mattered back then. As I sat in front of my desk with my deed to the property in my hand, I wondered if this was the kind of love Chris meant when he talked about the Fruit of the Spirit. Or maybe it was kindness. Or maybe it was both.

# Chapter 9: Leslie

"**Y**OU WANT TO GIVE me your land for the affordable housing project?" I leaned against the kitchen sink, shocked at Candy's words. Her land was valued at several million dollars and would have retired her if her music career didn't pan out the way she wanted.

"Mom, you're helping me chase my dreams." Candy hugged me around my waist. "Let's get yours."

A lump formed in my throat as I felt her arms around me. I'd have to think about it. "Okay," I managed. I wanted to give her the farmland in return, but knew the value was only half as much as what she was giving me. The Willis Farm had nothing but stubble, unlike the wide-open space in a cozy corner of Honeybrook, just minutes from the beach.

"The parcel is on the outskirts of Honeybrook, and it touches New Hope." I leaned against the counter, thinking about it more. "I'm not sure if the mayor will approve this, but we can try," I said slowly, knowing Rosewater would throw his weight around.

"Why not?" Candy zipped up her guitar and tossed it over her shoulder. She swung her backpack over her other shoulder and walked out the door. She was my heart and that heart of hers kept growing.

"You wanted to meet with me?" Mayor Rosewater sat across from me and Candy in my home office that Wednesday. I wished Chris was here. I had to maintain a level of professionalism, even if Rosewater did unnerve me and I still didn't believe his story. I had to carry on "business as usual" until the police finished their investigation anyway.

"Actually, Candy had some business ideas she wanted to share with you." I gave Candy a soft rub on the back and nodded for her to speak.

"So, I know you don't want us to use the land Mom just got for affordable housing. What about my land?" Candy's confident stage voice filled me with an ounce of mama-pride.

"*You* have land?" The mayor wrinkled his nose at me, astonished.

"Yes." Candy didn't miss a beat. "The Granville property is mine. I'd like to propose we use it for affordable housing."

The mayor didn't answer her, but looked at me. "How much are you paying your child to say this?"

"Candy will be voting age before we know it, Mayor. Teens grow up on us fast." I twirled my chair a little. "This is all her idea."

"Teens," Mayor Rosewater huffed under his breath. "I know your mother told you about when she was a teenager." The mayor leaned across the table toward Candy, who, to my surprise, brazenly stared back at him.

"Yes." Candy blinked twice, and I placed one hand on the desk in case he crossed the line.

"If this *is* your idea, why should I do anything nice after your family hurt mine?" The mayor asked the painful question, and my heart skipped a beat. My father had his son killed, but wasn't it enough revenge when he killed my parents?

"Jesus says to love." Candy's voice quivered as she spoke. "And He tells us to be kind and show goodness. If we have a problem in Honeybrook where our neighbors don't have a place to live, we're not loving at all."

"You're really too young for this kind of thing. Where is the Granville property, anyway?"

"On the water's edge on the outskirts of Honeybrook," I answered for Candy.

"Waterfront property!" The mayor completely removed his coat and slung it over the arm of the chair.

I picked up my readers and opened my laptop. I pulled up a document I'd researched on the town ordinances, where Candy wouldn't be too young if I cosigned her request to use the land for affordable housing. I turned the laptop towards the mayor.

"I'm sure you're familiar with this document," I said.

"Yes, I'm familiar. I don't have to grant you zoning, kid," Mayor Rosewater said to Candy. "I'll deny your request just as easily as I denied your mother's."

"Mayor, this is the outskirts, not the center of Honeybrook," I coaxed.

"Please don't say no," Candy begged, and suddenly the office felt very dark and warm.

I switched on the floor lamp next to me, but it didn't seem to help much.

"I might let you take a shot at it." Mayor Rosewater twisted his lips in a self-satisfied smile toward me. "I ran into Chris Schaeffer at the grocery store last night. The alleged robbery came up, but he told me your mother remembered nothing. If that's true, maybe we could talk."

Over the last few days, pieces of the painful night had started to return. The bruises at the hospital came later and I couldn't explain them, but the police wrote them down as the fall. Today, I remembered him upstairs going through my items a second time. I noticed more than the postcards were missing. Even though my memory was still shaky, I undoubtedly blamed him. He had my evidence, my clues about my dad, my pictures of my mom, everything! And now, he was forcing me into silence because I'd had the trauma-induced memory loss and he didn't.

Candy looked at me with hopeful eyes, and for the second time within a few months, I felt eighteen again. I wanted to do the right thing, to fix everything my dad had started. But I also wanted my items back and to find out about my dad's occupation.

"I don't remember much from that night, truly." I played along. "But if I get zoning, maybe you can use your political influence to help me regain my items. It would definitely help me feel better after all this."

The mayor locked eyes with me.

"Mayor," I said softly, "I can't call off the investigation, but I told the police that I'd press charges against whoever hurt me. I can drop any and all charges. My memory isn't going to improve in a few days." Those words cued the mayor into the fact that maybe I remembered an ounce of something–the very things he didn't want me to. He drew in a breath and stared at me. Our eyes traveled down to the bruises on my wrist.

"Then we have a deal." Mayor Rosewater reached across the table. "Affordable housing on the outskirts and confusing, forgotten nights, nothing else. I have enough political pull to see what I can do about your missing items."

I released a sigh of relief. For now, Jeremy stayed in the past, and Honeybrook finally got affordable housing.

My heart skipped a beat, and I placed one hand on Candy's shoulders. I had forgotten memories for the greater good. If the police found anything, I'd have to say it was a misunderstanding. But I still needed to know what my dad did for a living. As a new Christian, I knew when I did find out the truth about my dad, I might have to truly apologize on his behalf. But for now, I'd only staved the mayor off for a little longer.

"Congrats on your first land deal, kid. Chancellor Homes will receive the zoning agreement in the mail." Mayor Rosewater stood to leave, and I followed him out the door.

"What?" The mayor looked at me as I folded my arms against the wind. The darkened sky made him seem that much more ominous as he stood on the steps.

I thought about the scar below my ribcage that had never gone away after Jeremy's brutal attack. I thought about how my life could have been different if my parents had stayed alive, raised me fully, and kept me from drinking and smoking. Maybe my mother would have helped me during my pregnancies so I didn't feel anxious. I'd never know. And standing in front of the man who took her and my dad away from me, I bit my lip. Raindrops started to fall, and I looked Rosewater right in the eye.

"Have a good afternoon," I said and turned to go back inside.

The old man frowned and reached out a hand towards me, but I instinctively jerked away.

"A deal's a deal," I continued. "We'll wait for everything in the mail."

"Of course." Mayor Rosewater shuffled down the walkway, his coat slowly collecting raindrops.

I took in the earthy scent of the storm, then walked back inside to check on Candy.

"You did a good job, honey." I hugged her. "I'm proud of you and your dad would have been too."

"Helping like Jesus would, right?" she asked me.

I paused for a moment before answering, "Yeah, we're helping others." Having been a believer for almost a month, I wasn't sure if Jesus would have agreed with the mayor on a somewhat dirty deal, but I hoped He would find our hearts in the right place.

❧ ⸺ ◆ ⸺ ❧

"Let's try accessing your memories again." Trish sat in my office right before lunch. "Trauma-induced memory gaps happen, but as a part of your healing, it's important to try to recover what you can."

"It's coming back in spots, and I remember so much more now." I reached for my coffee. "Rosewater took my postcards, hit me, threatened me and my child, took my photo album, and behaved disgracefully after breaking into my home."

Trish's jaw dropped. "Why didn't you say anything, Leslie?"

I took a sip of coffee and tried to collect the right words. "Trish, the Rosewaters and I have—let's say..." I stirred my iced coffee with my straw a little. "An interesting history. I don't trust him. I needed the mayor's approval for zoning to finish the dream of my late husband. The town needs affordable housing. The only way those dreams could come true..." I put my cup down and leaned back in my chair. "If I forgot, everyone could start over. Only God, the mayor, and I know the truth. And I took myself out of the equation."

Trish twisted one of her dred locs and shifted in her chair. "How do you justify this in regards to your faith?"

I bit my lip. "I wanted to help others, help my daughter, and stay safe, you know? I mean, I truly forgot in the moment. Maybe when the moment is right, the mayor and I can have an honest conversation, but for now, maybe we can have peace?"

Trish gave me a side glance. "When is the right moment, Leslie?"

I leaned forward, frustrated by her interrogation. "I'm not trying to live in the gray." Irritation rose within me. "I'll come forward with the whole story when I actually know the whole story about my father. Until then, I won't go public with anything. I have to believe he had a reason to do what he did. Until I have the facts, there will be no comment. How do I even know I haven't forgotten anything else?"

Trish raised her eyebrows at me. "How does this make you feel?"

My frustration disappeared, and the new light in me stirred. "That maybe I should start reading the Bible for more answers and maybe the Holy Spirit will guide me to the next place to search." I didn't expect firm faith to come from my lips, but I'd hit rock bottom and came resurfaced with God's grace. I wanted to use that grace for good.

# Chapter 10: Candy

NINA, SCOTT, AND I practiced for our single almost every night, but tonight, Mom sat in the studio listening to us perform. I was also surprised but grateful Nate wanted to stick around and join us too.

"You guys sound great," Mom said.

"Thanks." I smiled at her.

Chris beamed at us. "This is the best group I've taught in my whole career."

I grinned at Scott, excitement racing through me. We recorded the single tomorrow!

❧ — ◆ ◆ ◆ — ☙

Later the next day—after I learned that the first day of recording is all sound checks and no actual singing—the police met with me and mom at the house with their findings. They suggested that the mayor didn't break in, but acknowledged that items had been stolen. But since I'd said someone who looked like the mayor had crept out our window, he was still on the short list. There were no photo albums or postcards at the mayor's house, his office, or anywhere to be found.

Mom sat at the table and offered the officers sandwiches and sweet tea as they filled her in with a few details. Her acquiescence blew me as she accepted the news without fighting back. It's as if she knew Jesus had the facts, and she didn't need more than that. In that moment, I learned that some people, like me, took time to grow. Others grew quietly and formed deeper roots, but then blossomed at just the right moment. That was my mom. She'd accepted Jesus, and when she needed Him, He was there.

He'd helped me and Mom grow past our struggles and had walked us through the scorching flames. Even though Mom told her version of the truth since her memory of the night was, in fact, sketchy, Jesus would always know. Mom showed the officers her bruises from her fall, but she didn't push too hard on the details. She did so for the sake of our safety and helping others. It all worked out. God does that sometimes, I realized. He works things out in the ways I never would have expected.

# Chapter 11: Candy

"GOD PLANTS SEEDS IN our hearts and makes them grow..." I sang into the mic softly.

Everyone in the studio clapped.

The second day of recording came to a close.

"Candy, if this single goes over well," Grayson Lee said as he walked over to my mic, "I think you should make an album."

I flushed. "Do you really think that Born Again would sign me on?" I asked.

"I don't see why not." Grayson was much taller than me, but he looked me straight in the eyes. "I haven't heard passion like yours since Rayne Nicole."

*Rayne Nicole!* I thought. *Rayne Nicole who'd won a Grammy last year?! And starred in a movie?*

"Thank you," I stuttered. Scott and I locked eyes and smiled. How could life look amazing like this, but somehow scary at the same time?

We continued to practice for hours at the studio and by the end of the week, the recording was complete. At the end of our last session, Chris and Mom clapped for us. Scott beamed. We finally had a single in the books. My heart brimmed with joy and it almost burst with gratitude. Despite all the trials, there'd been the triumph my heart had yearned for. *We the Guilty* would be back in a few weeks to record the second song where we'd be guest featured, since Grayson Lee had two concerts scheduled near Honeybrook.

"This is only the beginning, you know," Grayson Lee said to all of us at the door as he and the musicians started to leave. Mom, Chris, Nina, Nate and Scott stood with me. "Now, we have to see how the rest of the world likes the song."

My heart skipped a beat. *The rest of the world?!*

"And keep writing music from your heart." Grayson Lee shook my hand. "I'm hoping for your debut album."

My mind started spinning with excitement. "Of course," I said.

Scott placed a hand on my shoulder. After every single thing that had gone wrong, we'd made the single. Now those invisible red velvet curtains were pulling back as we began to share our new single with the world. For the first time in a long time, I had butterflies in my stomach. How would it go? And what would I do if it all backfired?

❧ ⋯ ◆ ⋯ ☙

Upstairs in my room the next morning, I worked on editing a song. I learned in science class that wildflowers bloomed in the winter and could yield fruit, which briefly made me think of the Fruit of the Spirit.

I scratched my head and reached for a scrunchie on my desk to tie back my hair. The words were forming in my head, but weren't coming together. I gazed at my ring from Scott on my hand and twisted it slowly. We'd grown so much. We'd literally survived a fire and still made a single.

I stood and left my room, my mind too cluttered to actually think of better lyrics for the one song that did dance in my heart. I'd named it "Wildflowers."

❯❯ ┄ ◆ ┄ ❮❮

Even though we'd been singing all week and we were all tired, singing our second song with Born Again Records–the one with Grayson Lee–was nothing short of a dream. We were home in our studio, but they brought the works. Born Again had connected us to makeup artists, sent us better cameras, and Grayson Lee gave me a professional level guitar–signed! It read: "Candy, keep on growing. Your bro in Christ, Grayson." I hugged the guitar tight to my chest as I got ready to play.

Mom sat in the room holding hot tea, and Chris stood in the corner beaming. Mrs. Carrington kept dabbing the corners of her eyes as Scott sat next to me on the guitar stool. Nina played with the practiced perfection we'd been working on. I closed my eyes as the memories of the last three months filled me. I'd made so many mistakes, but grace had covered me every time. The mistakes were like the dirt I needed to grow, and the pain had been water, because I'd already been a seed planted in Christ. The camera man motioned for me to start, and I strummed in sync with Scott. Our eyes met as I began to sing.

I hadn't expected the nervous pounding in my chest. The cameras weren't for YouTube, but still I loved it. I loved the moment when God heard my cry, answered my long-standing prayer with a yes and my dream began to become a reality.

Unlike our single, being featured with Grayson Lee took almost twice as long to get looks, shots, and sounds perfect. On the final day, with everyone gathered back in the studio, I held my signed guitar up close, sang the chorus, looked straight at the camera and stopped. I didn't know where my music dreams would take me. I could only pray for the best.

"Amazing!" Mom cheered after the cameras turned off.

"Way to go, guys," Chris said and gave me a hug.

Scott hugged me as we slid off the stools. We both went to hug Nina and high five Nate. The crew started to leave slowly, but Grayson Lee stayed behind.

"You did an amazing job today, Candy." The British accent seemed heavier this morning than usual. "Even if this doesn't make the top one hundred charts, keep singing. Keep praying, keep believing that every song for Jesus is touching someone's heart and it's worth it."

"Thank you for the chance to collab with you," I grinned. Seriously, we had a debut single *and* we were featured in *We the Guilty's* next song?

"We release next month," the producer from Born Again records said. "Start posting on social and we'll have a few concerts ready for you in a few weeks."

"She has to perform away again?" Mom nervously leaned forward and asked.

"That's a part of marketing," the producer said. "We promise we'll take good care of her."

Mom looked at me, and I could feel her usual anxiety rising. I didn't know how to feel. The mayor wasn't after us anymore, so there wasn't a problem, right?

Grayson Lee interjected, "Candy will only be performing concerts where she and her mother feel safe."

The Born Again producer looked at Grayson Lee, then Mom, then me. "You got it. But you two better be grateful you have talent. Anyone else, well..." he trailed off.

"Thank you." Mom walked over to the guitar stool and squeezed me close. "But wherever she goes, I'll at least be coming with her."

"Sure thing," the producer said.

He had no clue how much that meant coming from Mom. After so much loss, she was willing to believe and take a risk outside of Honeybrook again. My heart rejoiced with her, and I smiled at her. A single chance at making a single had proven to be a single glimpse into the glory of God.

# Chapter 12: Candy

"**Y**OU KNOW, I DIDN'T think the Fruit of the Spirit challenge would apply to me," I told Scott as we sat in an empty rec room for youth group, waiting for Chris and the others. "So much happened, I thought Mom and I should be receiving everything. And even when I thought I was already doing my best by being present–singing worship songs on stage–God showed me the other ways I should be bearing fruit."

I flipped my journal open and started jotting down the moments I had actually shown God's love.

"My family made peace with the mayor," I started. Scott wrapped one arm over my shoulder, and the metal chair creaked a little. "I've shown love to Mom as she's healing and joy onstage while we sang. I've shown kindness by giving up my land and faithfulness to my boyfriend, even when we were both hurting."

"I have to agree with all those things." Scott pecked me on the cheek. "You've truly turned into a flower."

"More like a wildflower."

Chris walked into the room and must have overheard us. "Don't let that smile trick you. She has a rogue streak straight from her mom. If you think you were showing kindness by posting on YouTube about the mayor, try again."

"I helped make peace," I explained.

"I'll take that, I guess." Chris gave me a smile as he sat down.

I laughed as more people entered the room.

"We're wrapping up the Fruit of the Spirit challenge," Chris began. "Does anyone feel as though they've practiced all nine?"

I listened as people talked about how they were patient with younger siblings, practiced self-control during sports, were kind to their grandparents, and dozens of other stories. But the flower in my heart seemed so special because Chris was right. I'd bloomed in a desert season of my life, making me a true wildflower. Only God could help me do that.

# Chapter 13: Leslie

I CURLED UP ON the couch with my journal in hand and twisted my pen as I thought about the coming months. We had a week before Easter, and I had more planning to do. The affordable homes wouldn't be built for months, but that wasn't a big deal. I wanted to personally allow Jack and his family to select where they wanted to live in the new community, especially after he'd been so helpful during my season of loss. Everything was finally settling into place. I couldn't believe we'd actually have an affordable housing community in Honeybrook. It had taken so many years, and if I were honest, it was the biggest and most meaningful project I'd ever undertaken. Rob's long-awaited dream was finally about to come true.

A text from Chris buzzed on my phone. **Dinner tonight?**

I smiled and texted back. **Sure.**

Candy had dinner with Scott that night, so Chris and I actually had the evening alone—a calm, quiet, uneventful evening.

"So, I know you still wear Rob's ring." Chris sat down next to me on the couch and motioned to my enormous diamond ring that had been resized. It had actually been my mother's, and since Rob didn't have the money for one, we used it.

"I don't want you to ever take it off," Chris continued. "When I asked you to walk with me to the end of the road of life, I never wanted you to forget where you came from."

I twisted my ring slightly, listening to his words.

Chris moved closer and put one arm around my shoulder, then removed it. "I only want you to wear this one on top." Chris fidgeted in his pocket and pulled out a small black box.

I opened it to find a simple, small diamond ring.

"I've known you forever." Chris leaned in for a kiss on my cheek. "But over the last few months, I've fallen in love with the fighter I'll love forever. How about it, Leslie?" he asked. "Will you marry me?"

I blinked back tears. "Of course." Somehow, in all my mess, I never thought Chris would ask so soon. He had the same feelings about me that I had about him—that soft, new love that was different than we'd ever shared before. I wasn't about to lose it.

Chris leaned over and kissed me softly on the cheek. "I love you, Leslie," he whispered.

"I love you too." I returned the soft kiss.

And there, in front of the flickering television screen, we held hands as my heart resumed a place of calm. I'd have love and support again, and I'd spend the rest of my life with the only man alive who knew me at my current best. My planning brain kicked into overdrive as I began to mentally prepare a wedding—my second wedding, but Chris' first.

We'd talked about walking to the end of the road together, so maybe a dreamy outdoor wedding? But then Chris said sunset, so orange, coral, or periwinkle? I felt myself growing more excited about the prospect of the wedding. I'd have to wear a completely new gown. I doubted I could still fit my old one. I smiled as I looked at him and he squeezed my hand. Life with Jesus and with Chris was a lot less lonely. And to some extent, it was less scary since I could tell myself Who was in control. Still, Chris and I hadn't settled on something very important.

"What do you think about being a dad?" I asked.

"Candy's a doll," Chris said.

"I mean a dad to a new baby," I said.

Chris moved back and studied me for a moment. "What do you mean?"

"Anna asked me to adopt her baby. I told her I would, but now that we're getting married, it's your decision too."

Chris paused, but only for a moment. "If you're comfortable with adopting Anna's baby, I'd be fine with it."

I hugged Chris. "I'm so glad. I want to, Chris. I need to hold a baby again," I admitted.

"Then it's the absolute right choice," Chris said and kissed me on the nose and we settled deeper into the couch. I stared at the flames of the flickering fireplace from the vintage movie, reminding me of how rocky the year had started, but how the spring had turned into something so much better.

<hr />

The next day, I drove to the site where the wrecking crew's machinery continued the demolition of my burned building. I couldn't walk onsite since the dust and fumes would wreak havoc on me, and I didn't have the equipment of my highly trained team. I had to sit in my car across the street and stare as my past shattered to the ground–Candy's home school room, the board room, my old mahogany desk, everything was gone for the most part. Rob's picture and a few family pictures had been saved. They were singed but saved. I ran my fingers over the steering wheel and turned up the heat in the car as the enormous wrecking ball moved to take another swing at the building. The men wearing yellow hardhats shouted commands from a distance.

I'd been saved too. Not just from the fire in the building, but from the fires of hell. With Jesus in my heart, I knew that for once I could rebuild. I didn't expect a single part of it to be easy, but I knew it would be possible and entirely worth it.

◆◈◆ ◆◆◆ ◆◈◆

"You want to adopt Anna's baby?" Candy looked at me with wide eyes at the dinner table.

Chris had a bad headache and hadn't joined us that evening. I thought he'd been working too hard, but I told myself I'd call him later.

"She really needs the support, and don't you think it would be nice to finally have a brother?" I asked.

Candy stiffened a little in her chair, and I wondered if I should have approached the subject in a different way. We'd been through so much and had so many things going on, I thought I had time to talk through her feelings about it later. But, by Candy's expression, I was on thin ice.

"Honey," I said, reaching for her hand. "I'm not going to have any more babies." I sighed and placed my fork on my empty plate. "You are my one and only. You're the baby your dad and I dreamed for, hoped for, and even prayed for. Anna's baby will be a special addition to our family." Candy seemed only moderately convinced. "I didn't think you'd adopt."

"He needs a home, and Anna can't do it."

"Doesn't a baby feel like a lot?" Candy asked the one question I feared. With my health, her upcoming graduation from high school, the concerts promoting the single, and my job, would a court approve me as a mother?

"It feels like a second chance to give you a brother," I told her and stood up from the table. "But it will be up to the court to decide." I sighed as I tossed my paper plate in the trash, then walked back over to my precious angel. "Sweetheart, will you please open up your heart to just a baby, not 'Anna's baby?'" I used air quotes for emphasis.

Candy hung her head, and I saw huge tears sparkling on her cheeks. "She was so mean to me, Mom. I forgave her, but her baby?"

I left my chair and walked over to her. "Sweetheart, I'm sorry for how Anna treated you, and I'm sorry I wasn't there to intervene. We're not adopting Anna, though."

Candy laughed and swiped her eyes. "So, I'm going to get a brother?"

"If the court agrees and if he lives," I said the two factors I feared the most out loud and let them freeze in the air. I glanced at Candy again. Telling her about marrying Chris could be either assumed or it could wait until later.

She'd had enough for one day. She favored me in moments like this. When she questioned the future, her eyebrows tucked together in thought. I couldn't blame her though. I often questioned the future too.

# Chapter 14: Leslie

I KNEW THAT WHEN Chris and I married, we'd want to either renovate the house or downsize to a new one, giving this home to Candy. But for now, sitting in a guest room I'd selected for the nursery—with an oak crib across from me and a matching changing table on the opposite end—I fought a mix of emotions. I was decorating again. I dared to hope for a baby again. I squinted around the room, making notes of everything that needed to be done and what needed to be changed. I stood and moved the rocking chair further back, closer in the corner. I reached into the bag of items I ordered almost a week ago and pulled out a stuffed rabbit and sat it in the rocking chair, his tiny blue vest appearing perky and expectant.

Grief kicked me so hard in the chest as I watched the rocking chair move back and forth slightly after I placed the bunny in his new spot. I started crying, thinking about the four other times I'd decorated nurseries—the powder blue, the soft yellow, the cotton candy pink, and the beige ones that had been met with so much anxiety. I had lived in Candy's pink nursery, worried that something would go wrong, that God was delaying my pain. But He'd blessed me with a sweetheart. I glanced at the walls of the nursery, noting how they missed artwork. This one would be a soft green with cream undertones, I decided. I wondered if any of my children would have survived had I faced my problems head-on earlier, when Rob was still living. Did I deserve the pain I'd received? I couldn't contain the waterfall of tears and leaned against the crib as the sobs came harder with each memory and every "I'm sorry" from doctors and EMS workers.

"I'm sorry, God," I whispered taking on every ounce of guilt from my past–drinking, smoking, lost babies, unkind words to Jeremy, sending Rob to get takeout, everything. Part of me knew I was taking on a little more, but another part of me felt very responsible because I'd said those words about Jeremy just like I'd asked Rob to get dinner. "Please forgive me, Jesus," I prayed just above a whisper.

I had thought I'd never make it as a Christian. Maybe I'd been too pessimistic. I smoothed the tiny blanket and tried to take in a slow breath. Right when I didn't think I had what it took to be a Christian like Chris or to be a mother to a new baby, grace met me in all its glowing warmth.

I never thought Jesus would take time to visit a woman with a past like mine, to talk to a broken, messy heart like mine either. But there, in the unfinished nursery, He took off my worn jacket of shame and replaced it with what I could only call grace. And that felt more like a soft sweater. I looked down into the crib, imagining the little face that would hopefully look back at me.

"Thank You for making me Yours and for second chances," I prayed aloud, realizing God and I were talking way more than ever before. And for that, I was grateful.

# Chapter 15: Candy

Sitting on my guitar stool next to Scott was exactly what I imagined sitting on a cloud must feel like: Perfect. Nina sat at the piano while Mom and Chris occupied the two orange chairs. The floaty feeling stayed on my brain as we prepared for future concerts with Born Again Records. Even though I didn't think my whole "Wildflowers" song was perfect, it was one of many songs that had been planted in my heart over the last few weeks. Chris had suggested I take a shot at singing it. So, sitting with my guitar on my lap and my new lyrics dancing around in my head, I leaned into the mic and sang:

I don't have a huge garden/
I only have one flower/
Just one flower to offer to the King/
True it's all I have/
Maybe it's all I'll ever be/
But with one wildflower/
Let me bear fruit for eternity/
Oh, Jesus, I want You to have it all/
Every single blossom I'll ever bloom/
Every piece of fruit that I will ever bear/
I know it's just one flower/
But God with Your power/
I know You'll help me bear fruit for eternity /

I don't have a huge garden/
I only have one flower/
Just one flower to offer to the King/
A flower that blooms with grace/
A flower that'll run this race of life/
A flower that'll bear love for the world to see/
Just one wildflower

As I sang the words, I kept blinking to keep the tears away. I'd changed the lyrics for sure, because now I knew God helps people grow when they yield their hearts to Him. He helped me bear fruit, even if all I had was my six-string and a singing voice. The words meant so much more to me than they did weeks ago. Yeah, I wanted to be a country singer, but even if this moment promoting the single was the only chance I ever got, I was grateful for it. I wanted to put my Jesus first in helping Mom, standing for what's right, and getting closer to Scott. I wanted to honor God in my music and bear fruit. However God wanted me to do that, I was open to Him showing me and not me showing Him. I released my dreams into the palm of God's Hand and whispered the last line one more time, "Just one wildflower."

The holiness of the moment warmed me from head to toe and I squeezed my guitar a little tighter. *Wildflowers* would be the perfect title for this song. Maybe God had given me the flower I'd prayed to have–the stage.

# Chapter 16: Candy

U PSTAIRS IN MY ROOM that night, I noticed a tiny envelope on my pillow. It said: "Candy." A sticky note in front of it read: *I'm so proud of you, and your dad would be too. Love, Mom.*

I reached for it and pulled out a single, stiff piece of paper. Sitting on the edge of the bed, I turned on my lamp to better see the words written in Daddy's unmistakable scrawled handwriting.

*Dear Candy,*

*If you're reading this you're eighteen! Happy birthday, love. (Or by some off-chance you're not and I died, but let's hope not) I'm so proud of you, honey. As of writing this, you're twelve and outside playing the guitar and singing your heart out. Never stop using the gifts God has given you. Sometimes life feels like a deserted battlefield, a wasteland, and a desert with nothing in it at all. In those moments, pray, because then God has a way of showing you that even in the wasteland, the desert, or the dead of winter, He can grow wildflowers. As a boy, I used to give them to my mom. But now, God has given me a garden of beautiful wildflowers. You and your mom are my everything. Never let the music stop, even if it's just in your head or one day I'm listening from Heaven. You will always be my cowgirl and my princess.*

*Love, Dad*

I couldn't swallow. After all the commotion about Grandpa's note, there'd been one for me. I leaned back and stared off at the wall. Daddy knew about wildflowers. I hoped Jesus and Daddy were proud of this one here on earth. I clutched the letter closer to my chest, letting the grateful tears fall. I'd worshiped, prayed, stood for my faith, fought for my family, and gave up my land for my fellow citizens. I wasn't the same girl anymore. I never would be.

Even when I was old and gray, I would never forget the winter when we made an amazing single, the feature we recorded over the past few days, or the fact that Born Again Records might let us make a debut album–even without the social media following they typically require. We'd record in the new studio Mom was building on the Willis farmland, if it was done in time. If not, Mom promised to be okay with us recording somewhere else. Chris took on the role of our paid manager and would have an entirely new job. He would be leaving Honey-brook High at the end of the school year, but told no one. I knew he'd be greatly missed by students, parents, and teachers alike. Everything kept changing.

It was like God saw that I yielded fruit and blessed me with the desires of my heart and the chance to yield more. And I'd take it. I wanted to collect all the flowers, bear the most fruit, and share it with the world. I slid Daddy's letter into our special travel journal and gave it a kiss before yanking the dangling light switch next to me.

The space under Mom's door was dark. I knew it had taken a lot for her to even put the letter on my pillow, so I didn't push it. I reached for my phone to text Scott.

**We might make an album!** I reminded him.

**I know. I'm so stoked.** Scott texted back.

**Do you think we have what it takes?** I texted.

Three dots floated across my phone screen, illuminating the darkness around me. I lowered my phone a little.

**God planted us here.** Scott texted. **So that means we have what it takes.**

**So, I guess that's what they mean by bloom where we're planted.** I sent it with a smiley emoji.

**Or something.** Scott wrote back.

I held my phone to my chest. Spring had sprung. I was about to bloom exactly where I was planted. This was the dreamy spot I'd prayed for, fought for amidst all the trials that had come in the span of three months. I only hoped I'd make God smile all the while.

# Also by Samantha Roman

www.ingramcontent.com/pod-product-compliance
Lightning Source LLC
LaVergne TN
LVHW041212080426
835508LV00011B/919